Eudora Welty: A Form of Thanks

Eudora Welty: *A FORM OF THANKS*

Essays by:
CLEANTH BROOKS
MICHAEL KREYLING
PEGGY W. PRENSHAW
WILLIAM JAY SMITH
NOEL POLK
REYNOLDS PRICE
CHARLOTTE CAPERS

Edited by:
LOUIS DOLLARHIDE AND
ANN J. ABADIE

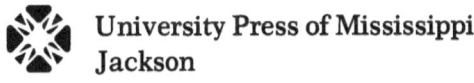 University Press of Mississippi
Jackson

This volume is authorized and sponsored by the
University of Mississippi

Library of Congress Cataloging in Publication Data
Main entry under title:

Eudora Welty : a form of thanks

   1. Welty, Eudora, 1909–   —Addresses, essays, lectures.
2. Novelists, American—20th century—Biography—Addresses, essays, lectures.   I. Brooks, Cleanth, 1906–   II. Abadie,
Ann J.   III. Dollarhide, Louis.
PS3545.E6Z66   813'.5'2   78–13285
ISBN: 978-1-61703-212-7

THIS VOLUME IS DEDICATED TO
EUDORA WELTY
AS
A FORM OF THANKS

Contents

Introduction

To inaugurate the Center for the Study of Southern Culture, the University of Mississippi on November 10–12, 1977, held a symposium honoring Eudora Welty, Mississippi's greatest living author. Attended by over 800 admirers, including students, faculty, and staff, and nearly 300 visitors from thirty-two states and three foreign countries, the symposium offered both serious appraisals of Welty's work by scholars and fellow writers and entertainment in the form of a dramatization of her novel *The Ponder Heart*, a reception and exhibition of some of her photographs, and a reading by the author herself. The presence of Miss Welty at all functions held over the three days added grace and meaning to all that was done and said.

At the peak of a career that extends from her first published short story, "Death of a Traveling Salesman," in *Manuscript* in 1939 to her Pulitzer Prize novel *The Optimist's Daughter* in 1972, Eudora Welty is today one of the most highly regarded of American writers not only in her native South, but throughout the United States and abroad. She has received every major award this country offers for exceptional fiction. A writer's writer, Welty has nevertheless built up over the years a wide, discerning audience of admirers who value each of her stories for its unique exploration of the human condition and its careful artistry. And to consider this achievement the Welty symposium was called together.

Although the subjects for the papers delivered at the symposium were chosen independently by the speakers, by the end of the meeting a kind of progression and unity of themes had emerged.

To open the symposium, Cleanth Brooks chose to speak on "Eudora Welty and the Southern Idiom." Beginning with Welty's remarkable handling of Southern speech, "something other than a corruption of correct English," and praising her respect for "this vigorous folk dialect," Brooks broadened the range of his discussion from mere speech to include Welty's treatment of the folk culture of the South. There is, he emphasized, nothing unusual in the fact that Welty, one of the most sophisticated of writers, can write so convincingly about this folk culture. "She views it," he stated, with an "artist's proper detachment." She never condescends to it, sentimentalizes it, or "takes it with anything less than full artistic seriousness." "The genuine artist," Brooks concluded, "not only respects and admires the oral tradition, he knows how to use it, how to incorporate it into the written, and thus how to give it an enduring life. Eudora Welty is just such an artist, for in her work one finds a true wedding of the two diverse but not hostile traditions."

William Jay Smith, looking at Welty's work from the poet's point of view, related her to the great oral tradition of storytelling in his paper "Precision and Reticence: Eudora Welty's Poetic Vision." "The ancient storyteller," Smith began, "was a poet, and to hold the attention . . . he made use of those age-old rhythmic and incantatory devices that we find in folktales." Smith then extended his discussion to "the deeper metaphor-making genius that places Eudora Welty in the oldest tradition of the poet-storyteller." He noted that one should be precise about the thing he writes, and reticent about the detail. To illustrate this definition of "poetic vision," Smith gave what is probably the most cogent discussion of *The Optimist's Daughter* written thus far, one to which all succeeding discussions will have to return.

Broadening the subject from speech and the oral tradition, from folk tradition and poetic vision, Peggy Prenshaw attempted a definition of the relative position of man and woman in Welty's fictional world in her "Woman's World, Man's Place: The Fiction of Eudora Welty." Beginning with *Delta Wedding* and continuing to *Losing Battles* and *The Optimist's Daughter*, Prenshaw maintained that the relationships, while not antithetical, are weighted with responsibility on the woman's side.

From Welty's handling of the relationship of the sexes, the symposium turned to her treatment of love with Noel E. Polk's "Water, Wanderers, and Weddings: Love in Eudora Welty." Focusing on the collection of stories *The Bride of the Innisfallen* and enlarging his consideration to later fiction, Polk defined "water" as "the matrix, our nourishment and our source of life . . . it is mysterious and fraught with peril." "Weddings" were seen as "not just the panoplied ceremony itself . . . but the entire spectrum of things having to do with love relationships"; "wanderers" are "people far from home and looking for something." "Water" may join or separate just as "weddings" may join and fail. The "wanderer" is one whom love has failed or who has in some way failed love. But, Polk concluded, love in Welty's work is "the source at once of the joy as well as the sorrow . . . that puts Miss Welty's characters into motion—the search for and retreat from love in any of its many forms, which manage to make us all wanderers on this earth, and all too frequently aliens in our own homes."

Then, centering on one work, a work combining the various themes of the folk, Welty's poetic vision, man and woman, and love, Michael Kreyling spoke on "Clement and the Indians: Pastoral and History in *The Robber Bridegroom*." Unhappy with early reviews of the novella, Kreyling undertook to call new attention to the deeper significance of Welty's fairy tale of the Natchez Trace. A "serious issue" raised in the work, he noted, is the "validity of history and of its arch-rival pastoral as claimants for human credence and trust." In *The Robber Bridegroom* Welty mingles both, but in such a selective and imaginative way that truth is the product of this strange merger. Both Clement and the Indians, pastoral and history, are valid claimants for human belief.

The final speaker, novelist Reynolds Price, delivered a tribute to Eudora Welty, "A Form of Thanks," that reiterated what he felt she has done for writers coming after her—"the gift of hope and instruction for another generation of American writers." Price concluded with a "gift" of a poem for her.

Not all the time of the celebration was given over to serious critical speculation. On the evening of November 10, the Department of Speech and Theatre of the University of Mississippi presented *The Ponder Heart*, a dramatization by the late Frank Hains that is feelingly close to the novel itself. For the production, directed by James E. Schollenberger, Jane Petty, who had appeared as Edna Earle in two earlier productions, came from Jackson to play the leading role once more.

A reception, centered around Patti Carr Black's exhibition of Welty's photographs, was held the evening of November 11 in the Kate A. Skipwith Museum of the University. Here participants met and talked with the author, who, until she tired, autographed books for them. The exhibition included photographs chosen by Black from the many negatives in the Welty collection housed in the Mississippi State Archives in Jackson, photographs Welty herself took in the 1930s.

The greatest pleasure, of course, was saved for last, when Eudora Welty read for a crowd of some 900 participants and visitors. Charlotte Capers introduced the author from the point of view of a friend. In her opening sentence, Capers promised a change of pace from the serious considerations of the days before. Then she recounted, with appropriate "odes," some celebrations held over the years among Welty and her friends, suggesting for those who have not had the privilege to know her, the lighter, *living* side of Eudora Welty. As Capers said, "There had been laughter and the love of friends."

Then, Eudora Welty read. As she read, the events of the previous days seemed to fall into place, to come into focus. As she read passages from her *Losing Battles*, her voice shaping each phrase as the living word, one remembered Cleanth Brooks's appreciation of her mastery of Southern speech and her truthful handling of the folk. One remembered Michael Kreyling's respectful regard for the artistic integrity of *The Robber Bridegroom*; Peggy Prenshaw's definition of the relative places of male and female characters—and from *Losing Battles*, how much it is a

woman's world; William Jay Smith's sensitive evalua-
tion of Welty's metaphoric, poetic vision; Noel E. Polk's
examination of love in her fiction; and Reynolds Price's
expression of thanks and his gift of a poem. Words and
phrases like "rich and exuberant talk," "variety of voices,"
"sustaining power of the humor," "matrix" as applied both
to woman's world and to the author herself, "outsiders,"
and everywhere "love" and "laughter"—all came back as
the Beechams and Renfros, Jack and Gloria, even hapless
Judge Moody and his wife, literally talked themselves to
life. It was amply clear that Eudora Welty's characters live,
and live beautifully, but they live to their fullest in the
sound of her own voice.

Her reading all too soon over, the symposium, like birthday celebrations, family reunions, weddings—all things
happy and life-giving—came to a close.

In preparing for the symposium many people and units
of the University were involved. The Center for the Study
of Southern Culture sponsored the meeting in coopera-
tion with the Department of English, the Department of
Speech and Theatre, the University Museums, the University Library, and the Division of Continuing Education.
In the actual planning of the program, English professors
Evans Harrington, director of the annual Faulkner Con-
ference since its inception in 1974, and Thomas H. Brown
gave freely of both time and much needed advice. The
Mississippi State Department of Archives and History and
Patti Carr Black, who put the exhibition together, provided Welty's photographs. Valerie V. Braybrooke, director
of the University Museums, arranged for the hanging of
the exhibition and made the facilities of the Kate A. Skipwith Museum available for the reception. Jane Petty, for a

number of years an outstanding actress and a founder of New Stage in Jackson, came early and stayed late to portray Edna Earle in *The Ponder Heart.*

Louis Dollarhide
University of Mississippi
Oxford, Mississippi

Eudora Welty: A Form of Thanks

Eudora Welty
and the Southern Idiom

CLEANTH BROOKS

LIKE ANY OTHER WRITER, Eudora Welty speaks and writes the Queen's English, or, if you prefer, now that a Southerner occupies the White House, the President's English; and she is the author of works that make use of the resources of our language at its highest level. The interior life, the world of fantasy and imagination, is the subject matter of much of her fiction. Robert Penn Warren, in a fine essay on her earlier work, has stressed her treatment of the theme of isolation and her concern for characters cut off from the world, alienated and locked into their own subjectivity. I acknowledge this important aspect of her work and doubtless it will be fully discussed in some of the papers that we are to hear later at this symposium. But what I want to stress this afternoon is Miss Welty's treatment of the folk culture of the South. She evidently knows that culture intimately, and her stories make it plain that she is fascinated by it. Nevertheless, she views it with an artist's proper detachment. Like the good artist that she is, she never condescends to the folk culture or treats it with anything less than full artistic seriousness.

3

I repeat: she knows its language thoroughly. She has got the vocabulary right and she has caught perfectly the accent, the intonation, and the very rhythms. But I wonder whether you who sit before me now take this folk speech seriously enough—not that many of you have not heard it all your lives. But life-long familiarity may have bred contempt, or at least indifference. Allow me, then, a few minutes' digression in order to try to excite your interest in what lies, if not all around you, at least not too far away, either in time or in space.

The typical language of the Southern folk culture is, within limits, a dialect of considerable force and vitality. Moreover, it is not a deformed and debased version of the standard language—that is to say, a bastard offspring of "correct" English. Its roots go far back into the past, for it derives from a speech long extant in the British countryside. How can I make this point forcefully and yet concisely? It occurs to me that the best way in which to do this is to read to you from a little book published in 1860. The book, by the way, is something of a rarity. No copy exists in that vast repository of books, the British Museum, or, as it has now been renamed, the British Library.

The author of this little book, a sound scholar of his own time, decided to present the King James Version of The Song of Solomon as it would have been pronounced by the dialect speakers of his native county. Here is the way it goes.

1 De song of songs, dat is Solomon's.

2 Let him kiss me wud de kisses of his mouth; for yer love is better dan wine.

3 Cause of de smell of yer good intments, yer naum is lik intment tipped out; derefore de maidens love ye.

4 Drâh me: we wull run âhter ye: de king has brung me into

his chambers; we wull be glad and be jobal in ye; we wull remember yer love more dan wine; de upright love ye.

5 I be black, but comely, O ye dâhṭers of Jerusalem; as de tents of Kedar, as de hangins of Solomon.

6 Look not upan me, cause I be black, cause de sun has shoun upan me; my mother's childun was mad wud me; dey maüd me kipper of de vineyards; but my own vineyard I han't kipt.

So run the first six verses of Chapter I. Let me conclude with a few verses of the last chapter.

6 Set me lik a seal pon yer heart, lik a seal pon yer arm, for love is as strong as death, jalousy is as cruel as de graüv: de coals of it be coals of fire, dat has a most out-de-way flaüm.

7 Evers'much water caunt squench love, nor de floods caunt drawnd it: ef a man wud give all he's got in his house for love, it ud be looked upan as naun at all.

8 We've got a liddle sister, an she han't got no brestes; what shull we do for our sister when de dee comes dat she's spoke for? . . .

14 Make haüst, my beloved, an be lik a roe or a young hart from de mountains of spices.

Does some of this sound familiar to you? Doesn't it remind you of a certain Southern dialect? May not a few of the pronunciations be your very own today? I, for example, tend to say *liddle*, not *little*, a word in which my Yankee friends at Yale are careful to preserve the *t*, whereas I, Southern fashion, turn it into a *d*. I also call attention to the fact that the author of this little book has carefully marked words like *made*, *grave*, and *haste* to indicate a sound like that of the so-called Southern drawl—which isn't really a drawl but the addition of an extra vowel so that nearly every long vowel becomes a dipthong.

What is the dialect used in this little book? That of the county of Sussex, only some forty or fifty miles distant from London. Now, if the country people of Sussex were pronouncing the language in this fashion in 1860, they presumably pronounced it at least this broadly in 1660, some two hundred years earlier, when the great immigration to America was going on, not only from Sussex, of course, but from the neighboring counties to the east and to the west. Surely, many of those who came to the Southern states must have spoken dialects of this general type—that is, variants of the dialects of the southern end of the island of Great Britain.

Now, changes undoubtedly went on after the colonists arrived on these shores. Dialects from different counties of the old country must have jostled against each other, and some of their peculiarities were lost. Education later had its influence. Those whites who had been saying *de*, *dat*, and *derefore*—and I conjecture that a good many must have—began to say *the*, *that*, and *therefore*. But a good many of the black people, who had, perforce, to learn their English from white English speakers, continued to use the *d*- forms because they were for a long time deprived of formal education and so retained the pronunciation they had first learned.

Now let me pause to make plain what I am *not* saying. I am not asserting that the Southern dialect is simply the Sussex dialect or other county dialects transported intact to these shores. As I have said, changes occurred on this side of the Atlantic over the centuries. New words were added from other languages. There was evidently a good deal of innovation, especially in vocabulary. So the assertion that I am making here is really a rather modest one: namely, that the *pronunciation* of the speech of the

American South was rather heavily colored by forms from the county dialects of southeastern and southwestern England, and I would add that some *standard* English pronunciations of the seventeenth and eighteenth centuries, pronunciations which died out in England, continued to flourish in America. Unfortunately, we just don't know enough about the development of the American regional dialects to be very specific about the precise details of that development. But the basic derivation of our Southern *pronunciation* of English from the dialects of the southern counties of England seems inescapable.

In any case, the acuteness of Miss Welty's ear for dialect is astonishing. For example, I had for years thought that I was alone in having noticed that many Southerners pronounce *isn't* as *idn't* and *wasn't* as *wadn't*, turning the standard z sound into a d. That, by the way, is a very out-of-the-way development. P's easily change into b's, or f's into v's, or t's into d's, but a sibilant turned into a dental stop is rare indeed. Again, this peculiar pronunciation of *isn't* and *wasn't* is found, and apparently found only, here in the southern United States and in some of the southern counties of England. Imagine my surprise, therefore, to discover in reading "The Petrified Man" that Miss Welty had unerringly picked it up and recorded it, and for good measure had elsewhere recorded another curious z to d shift, one that I had failed to notice—*business* pronounced *bidness.*

Now, I'm not trying to turn Miss Welty into a dialect specialist, much less a scientific phonetician. She has had far more important business in hand than that. But her grasp of the Southern dialect does have its importance for her literary artistry, and that is one point I have wanted to establish. And I have wanted to accomplish something else: to get this audience to take more interest in Southern speech, particularly in that of the plain people of the South, and to respect it as having historical roots that go far back, deep into the English past. If you can think of the speech of the plain people of the South as being something other than a corruption of correct English and can become aware of the continuity of their speech with the language of Chaucer and Shakespeare, you may be better prepared to understand the respect for this vigorous folk dialect which Miss Welty exhibits in so much of her writing.

So much for my references to pronunciation, but I should point out that pronunciation is the least part of Miss Welty's interest and concern. She is far more interested in matters of vocabulary and of metaphor and idiom. She means to bring Southern folk speech alive on the page in all of its color, vigor, and raciness.

The finest instances of her handling of the speech of the Southern folk are to be found in *The Ponder Heart*, *Losing Battles*, and *The Optimist's Daughter*. They constitute at least the great sustained examples of her rendition of that speech. But I'm not forgetting some of her short stories—for example, "Why I Live at the P.O." or that wonderful story, "The Petrified Man."

The action of this last-named story is set in a small town. The speech that we hear there is raffish and vulgar in a pseudo-citified way. It is the chitchat of a rather cheap beauty parlor. The language in *Losing Battles*, on the other hand, is not at all vulgar or cheap. The characters in *Losing Batles* are rustic and unlettered, but each of them is as genuine as a handmade hickory kitchen chair, not in the least common or trashy.

On the other hand, the beautician named Leota who

dominates "The Petrified Man" is wonderfully vulgar, but she is also wonderful to listen to in the same way as are some of the shabbier characters in Chaucer's *Canterbury Tales*. If the beauty parlor as the town headquarters for female gossip has cheapened and coarsened Leota's mind and spirit, her moving into town has not yet quite sapped the vitality of her country-bred language. It surges on triumphantly, and Eudora Welty has reproduced Leota's manner to a nicety. Listen to her on the subject of Lady Evangeline, the mind reader: When a customer asks "Who's Lady Evangeline?" Leota is not slow to come up with an answer.

> Well, it's this mind reader they got in the freak show. Was real good. Lady Evangeline is her name, and if I had another dollar I wouldn't do a thing but have my other palm read. She had what Mrs. Pike said was the "sixth mind" but she had the worst manicure I ever saw on a living person.

In Leota's mind, a certain professional knowingness lives happily alongside utter naiveté. Does Leota really think that a reading of her other palm wouldn't duplicate the reading of the first? Or does she credit herself with a split personality—two quite different minds to be read, one attached to her right hand, the other to her left? Yet maybe Leota is—in a certain crazy way—right after all. Though Lady Evangeline calls herself a mind reader, what she actually reads are palms. In any case, Leota, as a beautician, can spot a poor manicure right across the room. The "worst manicure [she] ever saw on a living person" belongs to a woman who is constantly holding in her hand other people's hands.

Eudora Welty's delicate but powerful grasp of the speech of the country people of the South reminds me of what William Butler Yeats, the great Irish poet, remarked in an essay entitled "What Is 'Popular Poetry'?" Yeats carefully distinguished between popular poetry and the true poetry of the folk. Popular poetry, he argued, did not, in spite of all its pretenses, issue from the folk at all. Yeats saw it as essentially a middle-class phenomenon, and the typical "popular" poets were Longfellow, Mrs. Felicia Hemans, and the Sir Walter Scott of *Marmion* and *The Lady of the Lake*. The audience to which this popular poetry appealed was composed of "people who have unlearned the unwritten tradition which binds [together] the unlettered . . . [but] who have not learned the written tradition which has been established on the unwritten." It's a very acute discrimination. Popular poetry in this bad sense appeals to people who have discarded the age-old oral tradition of the folk ballad and the folk tale. But in repudiating the heritage of the unlettered, they have not taken the trouble to master the written tradition of the truly literate reader. Yeats believed that both the oral and the written tradition could be expected to yield literature. What he denied was that true literature ever could issue from that group which was neither one nor the other—writers who wrote for readers only superficially literate, readers who wanted their poems and stories clear and plain, easily moralized and easily understood.

Yeats here is not condescending to the literature of the folk. "There is only one kind of good poetry," he insists, and poetry both of the oral *and* the written tradition belong to it, for both are "strange and obscure, and unreal to all who have not understanding." Those ignoramuses who have not understanding are members of that in-between group who demand "manifest logic" and "clear rhetoric." Television addicts and subscribers to the Book-of-the-Month take notice! The ghost of William Butler Yeats is looking very sternly at you.

I believe that Yeats has a genuine point here, and one that applies to the folk literature of the South. The Southern folk culture is still vibrant and alive, and affords rich material for the gifted professional writer who respects it and knows how to make use of it. The dangers are two: first, that the writer will exploit folk material for cheap laughs and so produce merely a succession of Little Abners and Daisy Mays, caricatures that are appropriate to an Al Capp comic strip but have no place in genuine literature. The other danger is that the folk speaker in actual life, the country-bred man or woman who is steeped in the oral tradition, will become merely half-educated and lose the values that he now possesses without acquiring the virtues of true literacy.

I hope that I am properly understood here: I am not for keeping the country folk on reservations as if they were an endangered species to be preserved for the amusement and entertainment of us well educated people. Quite the contrary: I would like to see the country-bred attain to full literacy and a full spiritual development. But the danger is that in a world of cheap and often meretricious reading matter and television programs they will not attain full mental and spiritual development at all. They will more likely lose the genuine tradition that they have without gaining the riches of the great tradition.

Leota, I would judge, has already picked up some of the triviality and cheapness of her rather scruffy beauty parlor life. But she still keeps her hold on a live and vigorous tradition of expressive English. If it is not quite what Spenser called "a well of English undefiled," neither as it yet a mere mud puddle.

Wanda Fay, in *The Optimist's Daughter*, by contrast, has been severely damaged. But perhaps she was flawed from the first. To have come out of a folk culture is no guarantee of virtue. Indeed, one of the fundamental religious tenets of the Southern folk culture is the doctrine of Original Sin: nobody is saved naturally; we have all fallen and come short. At all events, Wanda Fay is clearly a shallow little vulgarian.

She marries the widower, Judge McKelva, a man of some distinction, much older than herself, a man who comes from a very different stratum of society. When the Judge dies, Wanda Fay creates a scene at the funeral. She leans over her husband's coffin and cries out, "Oh, Hon, get up, get out of there." In dying, the Judge has somehow betrayed her, and she screams, "Oh, Judge, how could you be so unfair to me?" Someone tries to calm her and urges her just to bid him goodbye with a farewell kiss. Instead, she fights off the friends surrounding her and throws "herself forward across the coffin onto the pillow, driving her lips without aim against the face under hers," and is dragged "back into the library," screaming.

After the return from the cemetery, Wanda Fay's mother tells her bereaved daughter:

"Well, you've done fine so far, Wanda Fay. I was proud of you today. And proud for you. That coffin made me wish I could have taken it right away from him and given it to Roscoe." [Roscoe is her dead husband.]

"Thank you," said Fay. "It was no bargain and I think that showed. . . ."

"You drew a large crowd, too," said Sis.

"I was satisfied with it," said Fay.

Judge McKelva's only child, his grown-up daughter Laurel, is appalled. Later on, after her young stepmother's departure, Laurel's friends feel free to comment on Wanda Fay's conduct, and they do so. But Miss Adele Courtland, the school teacher and sister of the physician who attended Judge McKelva, tries to be charitable.

"Strangely enough, [she said] I think that carrying-on was Fay's idea of giving a sad occasion its due. She was rising to it, splendidly—By her lights! . . . She wanted nothing but the best for her husband's funeral, only the most expensive casket, the most choice cemetery plot, . . . and . . . the most broken-hearted, most distraught behavior she could manage on the part of the widow."

But her interpretation is not acclaimed. Miss Tennyson finally remarks savagely, "I could have broken her neck." We shall miss the point, however, if we conclude that Miss Welty means to disparage the yeoman whites as a class or even the lowly poor white. Wanda Fay is really awful: "common poor white trash" would scarcely seem too harsh a term to apply to her, and Wanda Fay's sister and mother are of the same stripe. But Miss Welty does not allow that even this family is wholly corrupted. Wanda Fay's grandfather, old Mr. Chisom, seems genuine enough, a decent old man, who had gone to considerable trouble to pay his respects. He arrives late for the funeral because he had had to make an all-night trip by bus. He has sat up most of the night shelling the prize pecans he is bringing to Laurel as a gift. He didn't mind the labor of shelling the pecans, he tells her; it was a way of keeping himself awake on the bus trip.

There is also little Wendell Chisom, attending the funeral in his cowboy suit. He sports a pair of holsters containing two toy pistols. Laurel, responding to the child's bewilderment and innocence, feels an impulse "to reach out for him, put her arms around him—to guard him. He was like a young, undriven, unfalsifying, unvindictive Fay."

The best testimony, however, to Miss Welty's respect for and even a certain affection for the genuine folk culture is to be found in *The Ponder Heart* and especially in *Losing Battles*. *The Ponder Heart* is comic, even merrily absurd; *Losing Battles*, though it has its own comedy too, and closes with a qualified happy ending, is more deeply grounded on the inexorable facts of life.

The Ponder Heart is in its presentation one long unbroken monologue issuing from the lips of Edna Earle Ponder, the proprietress of the Beulah Hotel, the main hostelry of Clay, Mississippi. Let no one object that Edna Earle isn't really one of the folk since she has deserted the countryside and become a townie, subject to some of the corruptions of a citified existence. In the first place, Clay is evidently not very much of a town. It merges easily into the country. The inhabitants of Clay are, to all intents and purposes, as Edna Earle would say, still country people. I admit that she is capable of amiably putting someone down by advising him not to be "so small town." But that is part of the joke. If Clay isn't small town, what town is?

In any case, Edna Earle is uncommonly good company. In her exuberance and in her earthy complacency, she reminds me of Chaucer's Wife of Bath. Like the Wife, Edna Earle is perceptive, on occasion even witty, and always the complete mistress of her own little domain. And like the Wife of Bath, how Edna Earle can talk! It is interesting to note what she says to her auditor as the narrative opens.

"*You're* here [that is, here at the Beulah Hotel, she tells him] because your car broke down, and I'm afraid you're allowing a Bodkin to fix it." [The Bodkin family is obviously in Edna Earle's black book.]

Is this remark a warning or a bit of commiseration? In any case, the man with the disabled car seems willing to let the subject drop; he has evidently picked up a magazine or a book, for Edna Earle immediately says: "And listen: if you read, you'll just put your eyes out. Let's just talk."

Edna Earle compels a hearing even as Coleridge's Ancient Mariner did, and like the Ancient Mariner she evidently does all the talking. Whether her victim eventually leaves her as a wiser and a sadder man, we do not learn. But one fact becomes plain: Edna Earle is clearly not a devotee of Yeats's written tradition. Reading just puts your eyes out. She is a high priestess of the oral tradition.

Someone has said that the many clichés and trite expressions that Miss Welty's characters, including Edna Earle, employ "reflect unimaginative thinking and [a] distrust of the new. . . ." To give an example, Edna Earle rattles off glib comparisons such as "she was shallow as they come," she was as "pretty as a doll," "he ate me out of house and home," "good as gold," could "cut your hair to a fare-ye-well," "didn't bother her one whit," and so on. These are well-worn phrases, but all oral art makes use of such formulas and couldn't proceed without them. The English and Scottish folk ballads are filled with such conventional phrases, and even Homer in his *Iliad* uses over and over again such formulas as "the rosy-fingered dawn" and "the fleet-footed Achilles."

Another critic may ask: "Don't her people often use

literary words that are quite out of character with their usual vocabulary?" For example, Edna Earle Ponder conjectures that "Maybe anybody's heart would *quail*, trying to keep up with Uncle Daniel's." Jack Renfro asks his father, "What brought you forth?" and tells Judge and Mrs. Judge Moody that "Banner is still my realm." How did these bookish terms, "quail" and "realm," not to mention "brought forth," get into the folk speech? Easy as pie, as Edna Earle would say. Right out of the King James Version of the Bible, or out of the hymns sung every Sunday morning in the Methodist and Baptist churches. If we need a reminder of the latter source, Miss Welty makes verses from the popular evangelical hymns resound again and again through the pages of *Losing Battles*.

A moment ago I mentioned the use of the word *whit* to mean a particle, a tiny bit. I remember my own mother's frequent use of the term. But just to be sure of the status of this word, I took the precaution of looking it up in the *Oxford English Dictionary*. It is a good English term going back as early as the fifteenth century, but the *OED* characterizes it as "now archaic or literary"; and this designation, it appears to me, is an excellent description of much of the vocabulary of the Southern folk speech such as one finds in the pages of Eudora Welty. The words are pleasantly out of date and may in fact sound "literary" just because they are not the ordinary speech of everyday as we hear it typically on national television or read it in *Time* magazine.

So much for what I trust may be my last digression. It's high time to get back to Edna Earle. Eudora Welty is an artist, and she has permitted Edna Earle to be a kind of artist too. In proof, listen to Edna Earle's summary account of her addle–pated Uncle Daniel's marriage to Miss Teacake Magee.

At any rate, Uncle Daniel and Miss Teacake got married. I just asked her for recipes enough times, and told her the real secret of cheese straws—beat it three hundred strokes—and took back a few unimportant things I've said about the Baptists. The wedding was at the Sistrunks', in the music room, and Miss Teacake insisted on singing at her own wedding—sang "The Sweetest Story Ever Told."

This is masterly.

Losing Battles is Miss Welty's most profound and most powerfully moving account of the folk society. In it we listen to a whole clan gathered for the birthday of its matriarch, great-grandmother Vaughan, and we hear them talk from the dawn of one day to near midnight and later on into the afternoon of the following day. It is wonderfully rich and exuberant talk and there are a variety of voices: male and female, gentle and quiet or aggressive and domineering, querulous and argumentative or ironic and conciliatory; but they are all voices of the folk and speak the characteristic folly or wisdom, joy or melancholy, of such a community.

In emphasizing the wonderful talk to be found in this novel—its quality and its quantity—I may have given the impression that nothing happens—that the novel is all just talk. Nothing could be further from the truth. All kinds of things happen. There are hairbreadth escapes from violent death, turnings of the table in which the judge who had sentenced Jack Renfro to the penitentiary turns up, through a curious set of happenings, at Granny Vaughan's birthday party for the concluding banquet and actually spends the night under the same roof that shelters Jack Renfro on his first night home after returning from the penitentiary. Mysteries are unraveled: Jack's bride, Gloria, the orphan who does not know who her parents were, has the puzzle worked out for her and discovers that she is her husband's first cousin. But as she is welcomed into the clan as blood-kin, no longer just an in-law, it is revealed that Mississippi has passed a law against first cousins marrying each other. Gloom descends at once. Will Jack, just home, have to return to the penitentiary because of this newly discovered offense? He had earlier had to give up his bride after only one night of married bliss. Now that he has held her in his arms once again, will he be snatched away? Yet it is his old antagonist, Judge Moody, who enables him to escape this new threat of the law.

I am reminded here of some amusing anecdotes that my wife recently passed on to me—anecdotes of which she was reminded by reading *Losing Battles*. During World War II, when she worked at a small war plant, she acquired a secretary from East Feliciana Parish, Louisiana, a young woman probably from just such a family as the Renfros. The secretary had obviously "risen," as had Jack Renfro's young wife, Gloria. She was not in the least self-conscious about her background, though now living a more sophisticated life in Baton Rouge.

During the Christmas season, she spoke of her pleasure in seeing her two young brothers, home on leave after having been away for some months. Not in the Army, it turned out, but in the penitentiary—for what offense I don't know, but probably something not very shame-making. They had brought along with them an obligation—and not just the obligation to return to the penitentiary when leave was over. Their particular task—one for which presumably they possessed talent—was the care of the penitentiary bloodhounds. They had done such a good job in taking care of, and possibly training, these dogs that they had been required to take the bloodhounds along on Christmas leave and care for them at home. The fact that the Louisiana State Penitentiary is located in the same parish in which the boys lived makes the happening more logical. They probably knew the warden or other employees, probably had uncles and cousins on the staff; so the particulars of their Christmas leave were easily and naturally arranged.

Another anecdote from my wife: the secretary wanted to take an aspirin; yet the only source of water was the office drinking fountain—no glasses or paper cups. She was at a loss. My wife suggested that she put the aspirin in her mouth and then drink like a chicken. There was instant communication and the aspirin were successfully swallowed.

But back to *Losing Battles*. Action, indeed! Far from being simply a talky novel, *Losing Battles* is practically a melodrama—and thus far I have not even mentioned the violent physical action, such as the fist fights that occur or the wonderful episode in which Judge Moody's car runs off the road and sits perched on an eminence so perilous that it takes truly superhuman efforts to get it down once more into the road.

The truth of the matter is that *Losing Battles* is in spirit a kind of Tall Tale of the Old Southwest. Indeed, the action is so violent and some of the coincidences so improbable that it needs its folk language and sayings and ways for the actions depicted to pass muster as credible. Pass muster they do, for by virtue of its folk characters and the language they speak, the novel strikes the reader as being itself a kind of folk tale—bardic, outrageously strange, almost epic in its happenings.

A second qualification that I want to make is this: in spite of the seriousness with which Eudora Welty takes this folk culture, she does not sentimentalize it. She does not make it too good to be true. If the clan loyalties of the Beechams and the Renfros are admirable and excite the envy of us modern readers who tend to be alienated, lacking in family ties, and lonely in our unhappy self-sufficiency, Miss Welty makes it plain that the pressure of this great extended Renfro family can be suffocating. Gloria wants to have Jack to herself. During his long absence she has tried to find a little privacy in this busy, cluttered, almost too tightly related tribe. Even after she has had revealed to her that her father was a Renfro too, she yearns to get away from Jack's vast family. As the novel ends, she is still saying: "And some day, some day, yet, we'll move to ourselves. And there'll be just you and me and Lady May." Lady May is their baby girl.

This counter note, this glimpse at the other side of the matter, is the necessary pinch of salt. The strength of family ties is touching, and the loyalties of the clan may well rouse in the modern a certain homesickness for a world that many of us have lost. But Miss Welty is not writing a tract in defense of the extended family. Rather, she is dramatizing such a family, and in doing so she is telling the truth about it. The virtues are there, but the Renfros have the defects of their virtues.

One of their defects is a kind of naiveté. Jack is good-hearted, impulsive, loyal, essentially kindly, though very jealous of what he regards as his masculine honor. It is his naiveté which first gets him into trouble, and in the course of the day and a half that we watch Jack's actions we see that his guileless simplicity continues to get him into trouble. His young wife Gloria is quite aware of this. She feels more protective of her husband than even he feels protective of her, for she realizes that he is far more vulnerable. He allows people to goad him into foolish actions. He is really incapable of taking care of himself.

Some of Jack's aunts and uncles and cousins are more worldly-wise than he. Yet in a sense Jack Renfro's special vulnerability does hint at the vulnerability of the folk society itself. It is genuine, sincere, strong in integrity, resolute, and capable of suffering without whining. But its chief virtues are those that can be handed down in a simple and basically unlettered society. Book learning, after all, does provide virtues too—very important ones— and these the Renfros tend to lack.

The folk society is a bit skittish about book learning. It is natural that it should eye with a certain suspicion the world of books and the rhetoric of false grandiloquence that goes with it. A little learning is indeed a dangerous thing, and on this point the suspicion manifested by the folk makes a certain sense. But the folk are even more afraid of profound learning—for this smacks of a strange and unfamiliar world filled with abstractions.

Miss Welty has made this point subtly but very forcibly in *Losing Battles*. Though we never see Miss Julia Mortimer, the school teacher who has made her impact on so many lives in Banner, the bailiwick of the Renfros, her name comes up again and again throughout the novel. She has just died. Indeed, her funeral is held the day after the Renfro reunion, and the whole community repairs to the cemetery to witness her burial. Judge Moody and his wife attend it, and so do Jack Renfro and Gloria. Gloria had in fact been a protégé of Miss Julia's and had come to the

Banner community as the mistress of its one-room school.
It was in the school that she met Jack, an overage pupil,
and fell in love with him, married him, and gave up the
career of a teacher, the profession to which Miss Julia had
hoped Gloria would devote her life.

Miss Julia had been a great teacher and a formidable
power in the community. Judge Moody, for example, had
been one of her pupils, and several of her best pupils had
gone on to glory in the great world outside. On the day of
her funeral men of more than merely local fame had returned to Banner to pay their respects. Yet in the talk that
we hear from the Renfro clan, we note a certain uneasi-
ness and suspicion. They respect Miss Julia and even take
some pride in having weathered their experiences in her
schoolroom. But they think of schooling as a necessary
evil, and their awe of Miss Julia is mingled with a certain
fear. She was the dedicated priestess of what was for them
an arcane mystery. They were never really comfortable
with her.

A folk community is usually uneasy in the presence of
those who exalt the written word, and in this regard Miss
Welty's Banner community is not special. Other Southern
writers have made the same point. An excellent example
is Peter Taylor's fine story "Miss Leonora When Last
Seen." The story is narrated by one of Miss Leonora's
former pupils, and in his account of this admirable but
formidable woman, who wished to lift her pupils to a
higher plane of intellect and achievement, the narrator
himself reveals mixed feelings. If in the end he comes
down firmly on Miss Leonora's side, his difficulties with
her schoolmarm-ism clearly reflect the mixed feelings of
the town. In *Losing Battles* this mingling of respect with a

certain resentment, and gratitude with fearful apprehension, comes to a head in the person of Gloria. Gloria owes much to Miss Julia, and yet she resents the fact that Miss Julia had not aproved her marriage to Jack Renfro. Gloria seems to count herself a brand snatched from the burning, a maiden rescued by her own St. George from the dragon of permanent spinsterhood. Yet, much as she loves her young husband and baby, she resists sinking back into the clannish domesticity of the Beechams and Renfros. She does want her own life as a wife and mother, but not on just any terms.

The suspicion in which any teacher is held by the generality of the folk—particularly their suspicion of the person who means to teach them how to read and write and spell—is not, however, merely Southern. I'm inclined to say that it is All-American. When I meet strangers and they find out that I'm a college professor, they invariably politely ask what I teach. I dread to tell them, for I can predict the chill that will immediately descend. "Gee, English was always my worst subject." Or: "You probably think my pronunciation is awful." Or perhaps, trying to cheer me up: "But you don't talk like an English professor. You sound perfectly natural."

Such is the uneasy truce that is struck between the representatives of the oral and the written traditions. And I can be sympathetic with the fears that plague the child of the oral tradition. He has good reason to guard his innocence. Thus the Renfros, who instinctively flinch from the sophistications of the great world outside, see the school teacher as the prime agent of that studiedly artificial world. As we have earlier remarked, Yeats believed that members of the unwritten oral tradition had cause to be wary in the presence of the evangelists of the printed word. But Yeats knew also that the genuine artist does not threaten the oral tradition of the folk.

The genuine artist, though aware of the limitations of the unwritten tradition, respects it. He appreciates its honesty and its other basic virtues. He knows that these virtues are not really antagonistic to the virtues of the great written tradition. He remembers that Homer, the father of the poetry of Western civilization, was himself a poet of the oral tradition, even though he was to become the very cornerstone of the written tradition.

The genuine artist not only respects and admires the oral tradition; he knows how to use it, how to incorporate it into the written, and thus how to give it an enduring life.

Eudora Welty is just such an artist, for in her work one finds a true wedding of the two diverse but not hostile traditions. It is as such an artist that I salute her on this happy occasion.

Clement and the Indians:
Pastoral and History in
The Robber Bridegroom

MICHAEL KREYLING

A SERIOUS ISSUE IS RAISED in *The Robber Bridegroom*: the validity of history and of its arch-rival pastoral as claimants for human credence and trust. We have, more or less, decided in favor of history. That is not to say that in so doing we have discovered the final truth of the issue. And it is the peculiar and fascinating nature of this short novel, *The Robber Bridegroom* (published in 1942 when this nation and most of the Western world were embroiled in, perhaps, more history than we would have liked) that history and pastoral and their perpetually unresolved rivalry are major thematic and stylistic elements, visible and audible in setting, character, and dialogue. The place, the people, and what they do and say, such basic ingredients of fiction, have been coaxed by the author to display their deepest and most far-reaching significance.

Hints of this rivalry have impressed readers of *The Robber Bridegroom* since its publication. Writing in *The New York Times Book Review*,[1] Marianne Hauser praised the

---

1. Marianne Hauser, "Miss Welty's Fairy Tale," *The New York Times Book Review*, 1 November 1942, pp. 6–7.

author's charming touch in cleverly blending fairy tale and ironic insight:

> It is a modern fairy tale, where irony and humor, outright non-sense, deep wisdom, and surrealistic extravaganza become a poetic unity through the power of a pure, exquisite style. . . .

Miss Hauser does not explore the wisdom further, nor give her reasons for qualifying "fairy tale" with "modern." She was writing a review, not an essay; and, moreover, we do not need much more explanation. We know that the irony makes the fairy tale modern. And we know the fairy tale is ours: the story of white settlers pursuing their dreams of a new world into the mysterious wilderness, which they proceed to subdue. Such has been our story as a nation since the first settlers in boats bumped the eastern coast. Irony, however, has been the lesson of history.

Lionel Trilling, also writing a review, looked askance at the whole thing:

> But its lucidity, its grace, and its simplicity have a quality that invalidates them all—they are too conscious, especially the simplicity, and nothing can be falser, more purple and "literary" than conscious simplicity.[2]

Alfred Kazin, on the other hand, trusted the seriousness of the novel. Acknowledging the style, humor, and fantasy present in the work, he noticed the author's theme moving beyond these elements:

> If this is an enchanted world, the black forest of childhood, it is also one into which the sadder, newer world is breaking. And the

---

2. Lionel Trilling, "American Fairy Tale," *The Nation*, 19 December 1942, p. 687.

slow, long roll of disenchantment can be heard at the end, where the Indians capture all the characters and decide their fate, as the axe that broke the trees only led the way for the machine that would break the forest.[3]

These few excerpts from reviews suggest that *The Robber Bridegroom* has from the outset left readers with two basic impressions: the amusement of a fairy tale retold with irony and the seriousness of an examination of the theme of disenchantment in the pursuit of a pastoral, and fundamentally American, Eden.

I have always been fascinated by the utterly different ways intelligent readers have reacted to *The Robber Bridegroom*, and I have concluded that the different reactions mean two things at least—that in literary criticism one usually if not infallibly ends where one's premises dictate, and that the mark of good literature is that its whole is undeniably greater than the sum of its parts. Leaving the dictations of literary critics' premises for another time, I want to talk about *The Robber Bridegroom* and to persuade you that in its wholeness it is much more than the sum of its parts, that indeed it possesses parts not usually or adequately noticed.

I realize now the dangers of overanalysis. *The Robber Bridegroom* is funny, and he who explains jokes kills them in the process. I do not want to explain any jokes. Nor do I want anyone to forget that *The Robber Bridegroom is* funny. Therefore I will tell my favorite jokes.

The first is a marvelous sight gag. (Deadpan lines from the lips of legendary figures, previously thought to utter nothing short of quotable truth or frontier boast, are the

3. Alfred Kazin, "An Enchanted World in America," *New York Herald Tribune Books*, 25 October 1942, p. 19.

lines that remain most hardy.) Rosamond, the damsel of the tale, has suffered the humiliation of being robbed of every stitch by the dashing bandit of the Natchez Trace. Is she flustered? Not for a second. She calmly returns home clothed only in her tresses and a straight face. Salome, her stepmother and a stern woman, demands to know the whereabouts of the herbs she had sent the feckless girl to gather in her apron. What herbs? What apron?

Another comic scene occurs when the hapless gnome of the story, Goat (an apt name since he not only has to butt his way into and out of things but is also the "goat" of Salome's foiled revenge plot against Rosamond) comes upon Rosamond weeping in the tent of her Indian captors:

"Good evening, why are you crying?"
"Oh, I have lost my husband, and he has lost me, and we are both tied up to be killed in the morning," she cried.
"Then cry on," said Goat, "for I never expect to hear a better reason."

Sometimes damsels are more aggravation than they are worth.

And yet another delightful exchange occurs when Rosamond, hugely pregnant with the hero's twins, has taken to the road to find Jamie, their father. She encounters Mike Fink, who has been exiled from the river for losing face to Jamie Lockhart in a fight. Fink, convinced that he has murdered Jamie, is just as sure that Jamie's ghost has come back to haunt him. Rosamond knows otherwise and tells Fink to notify said ghost, at his next materialization, that he is soon to be a father. "Oh," Fink said. "Ghosts are getting more powerful every day in these parts."

The sustaining power of the humor cannot be overstated. The wry, deadpan tone with which Miss Welty retells the legendary tale of the Natchez frontier propels the novel. In fact, the caricatures may be taken for the whole meaning of *The Robber Bridegroom*. Alfred Uhry, who has written book and lyrics for a musical adaptation of the novel, emphasizes this aspect. He omits the Indians as well as the serious aspects of Clement's character.

If jokes were all *The Robber Bridegroom* relied upon, then Lionel Trilling's objection on the grounds of simplicity could be readily allowed. This kind of humor can be too easy. But the novel is not limited, in its technique, just to the jokes. It reaches for something beyond the momentary relief of laughter. One laughs at Clement Musgrove much differently from the way one laughs at his silly daughter, or at her slightly ridiculous hero, or at her lavishly evil stepmother, or at any one of the menagerie of nuts who appear in the brief story. Clement is foolish in the way that Don Quixote is foolish. One laughs at them both with full sympathy, for the cruel, absurd, treacherous world they wrestle with, in innocent vanity, can never be subdued.

And besides Clement, there are the Indians, who spark something other than laughter. The Indians are re-created with a depth and quality of sympathy that Cooper sometimes, but not always, mustered. They are not the whooping stereotypes of greasepaint westerns. In the Natchez Indians of *The Robber Bridegroom* are found nobility, mystery, beauty, and pride. They are the spirit of the country. In fact, Clement and the Indians represent a different side of this light-hearted tale.

Miss Welty chose a real place for her "fairy tale"; this choice infuses *The Robber Bridegroom* with its undercurrent of irony and deliberate seriousness in which the Indians and Clement move. "Whatever is significant and whatever is tragic in a place," Miss Welty has written about the river country in which *The Robber Bridegroom* is set, "live as long as the place does, though they are unseen, and the new life will be built upon those things—regardless of commerce and the way of rivers and roads and other vagrancies."[4]

The real place Miss Welty chose for the setting of *The Robber Bridegroom*, Rodney, Mississippi, teems with this unseen life. Rodney began its history as a thriving town on the Mississippi River. Delta cotton went to market through its port, and Clement Musgrove's crop goes to New Orleans through Rodney. He and his money return through the town to begin the story. Sometime after the War Between the States, however, the river changed course and left Rodney a ghost town. That doom which occurred in history hovers in the future of the Rodney of the novel, shading the hijinks with a sentence of death. The place in which *The Robber Bridegroom* happens is both real and imaginary—the timeless land of fairy tale, and the changing world of historical and geographical event. Rodney is a ghost, symbolically cut adrift in time when the river went away and left it.

Rodney is not the only ghost whose presence tempers the "rollicking" novel with meditative seriousness. The Indians, who appear at the opening of the story and at the close, whom all the white pioneers fear as they fear the dark encircling wilderness itself, are both real and ghostly Indians. These Indians of *The Robber Bridegroom*, although their tribe is never named, are directly modelled

---

4. Eudora Welty, "Some Notes on River Country," *Harper's Bazaar*, February 1944, p. 156.

on the Natchez.[5] Although the history of the Natchez was finished years before the imagined events of the novel, the facts of their demise vibrate significantly as an undercurrent of the story.

The Natchez were massacred in 1730 in retaliation for a massacre of their own, and the remnants of the tribe were sold into slavery in Santo Domingo by the French in the eighteenth century. Besides their name, the Natchez left behind the vivid memory of their beauty, mystery, and pride, and Miss Welty has enlarged that memory:

> It is not strange to think that a unique nation among Indians lived in this beautiful country. The origin of the Natchez is still in mystery. But their people, five villages in the seventeenth century, were unique in this country and they were envied by the other younger nations—the Choctaws helped the French in their final dissolution. In Mississippi they were remnants surely of medievalism. They were proud and cruel, gentle-mannered and ironic, handsome, extremely tall, intellectual, elegant, pacific, and ruthless. Fire, death, sacrifice formed the spirit of the Natchez' worship. They did not now, however, make war.[6]

The Natchez, in a way, incarnate the spirit of this natural place, and they fell, as the place itself fell, before the advancing waves of Western civilization. Their residual spirit, like the echoes of a thriving Rodney, haunts the setting of *The Robber Bridegroom.* But not with a haunting so "mundane as a ghost."[7] The exterminated Natchez and

---

5. The source for this identification is Miss Welty's screenplay for *The Robber Bridegroom,* on deposit at the Department of Archives and History, Jackson, Mississippi. The screenplay specifically names the Natchez; it explains that they are the only "solecisms" in the cast, having been massacred in 1730. Used with permission.
6. Welty, "Some Notes on River Country," p. 153.
7. *Ibid.,* p. 86.

the faded town of Rodney haunt the so-called fairy tale with questions much more solemn than those of happy endings.

Time and events make ghosts of the Indians and the town, and these are forces neither the Indians nor the conquering white pioneers can control or foresee. Although the tale takes place in the abeyance of time, by choosing Rodney and the Natchez Indians, Miss Welty underscores our knowledge that, no matter what possibilities of wealth and empire the future may seem to offer, human time is finite; nothing man builds or accumulates is permanent against time. The Indians are in the throes of change and extinction; Rodney is a static omen of the same imminent change. The Indians' way of life and its passing dramatize the meaning of change; the presence of Rodney bodes it.

Another undercurrent in Miss Welty's use of the lost Natchez tribe is that change is not necessarily progress. In fact, it seems to be loss. The Indians inhabit the "enchanted forest" of the novel in a mysterious way that contrasts sharply with the noisy intrusion of the pioneers. This distinction is a facet of the pastoral theme: man's relationship to the earth is changing in time for the worse. The Indians enjoy an organic union with the place, appearing and dissolving in the surrounding forest, to the eyes of the pioneers, as if Indian nature were not restricted to merely "human," but partook of the animal and the vegetable as well. White men never spy the Indians first, but only after the Indians have chosen to be seen, when escape from a "reckoning" is impossible. Clement Musgrove's memory of his first captivity by the Indians expresses this pioneer astonishment at the Indians' mysterious oneness with the surrounding wilderness:

They showed their pleasure and their lack of surprise well enough, when we climbed and crept up to them as they waited on all fours, disguised in their bearskins and looking as fat as they could look, out from the head of the bluff.

The cunning art of disguise links the Indians intimately with their natural place. And the lack of it in the pioneers accentuates their estrangement from nature. Beyond the closed circle of their immediate, well-lighted camp, the pioneers enter an unknown universe. To them, the Indians are always lurking just beyond what can be clearly seen and controlled, and the image of the "encircling Indians" becomes married to all that the settlers fear: suffering, death, the unknown. Out of this fear comes the awful solution: The Indians must be eradicated.

The Robber Bridegroom, although a "fairy tale," and an enchanted story, acknowledges the torture and death and violence that the Indians inflict on the pioneers, and vice versa. This bloody violence was noted by John Peale Bishop in his review of the novel, but the theme of extinction and change did not fully occur to him.[8] Extinction and the fear of it are as much a part of *The Robber Bridegroom* as the cartoons, the borrowings from Grimm, and the frontier folklore. In fact, the violence plays an essential part, for this novel is properly a "local legend" and not simply a "fairy tale." As local legend it "has a personal immediacy, a cruelty, and a directness [which are] glossed over in the fairy tale."[9] The real place *was* violent, as well as beautiful, and violence was an indispensable part of the

---

8. John Peale Bishop, "The Violent Country," *The New Republic*, 16 November 1942, pp. 646–47.

9. Francis Lee Utley, introduction to *Once Upon a Time: On the Nature of Fairy Tales*, by Max Lüthi, tr. by Lee Chadeayne and Paul Gottwald (New York: Frederick Ungar Publishing Co., 1970), p. 16.

pioneering enterprise. Rodney was founded on violence; the Indians resisted violently and were crushed. This is the contradiction that maims the pastoral ideal: the maintenance of it requires violence, literal or figurative. And, finally, the means corrupt the end.

Our glimpse of the Indians while they are yet in their full pride, on the peak from which they are eventually pushed by civilization, is Clement's early life history, which he relates to Jamie Lockhart in the Rodney inn. Clement remembers the Indians as both gay and cruel, like the Natchez. But, as Jamie comments, "This must have been long ago . . . for they are not so fine now, and cannot do so much to prisoners as that." Once, supreme in their power over their captives, the Indians struck Clement with their imperiousness and fierce pride:

We had to go whirling and dizzied in a dance we had never suspected lay in our limbs. We had to be humiliated and tortured and enjoyed, and finally, with most precise formality, to be decreed upon. All of them put on their blazing feathers and stood looking us down as if we were little mice.

Then, with "scorn" the Indians put to death Clement's infant son, and with "contempt" dismissed him into the wilderness with the body of his first wife, Amalie.

Once the Indians were sovereign. Their realm was unfenced, unsurveyed, undivided. The onslaught of pioneers was but a trickle, and well within the Indians' power to stop. In this first "reckoning" episode of the novel, the Indians can decree and pronounce. The time is still their own.

Nevertheless, extinction is their fate. If Jamie Lockhart, the successful bandit and gentleman, has his way, the Indians will be eradicated like ants at his picnic. ("The savages are so clever they are liable to last out, no matter how we stamp upon them.") Clement, however, is not so vehement; vengeance does not consume him, even though he, not Jamie, has lost loved ones at the hands of the Indians. Rather, Clement contemplates the Indians' fate with a puzzled melancholy. His melancholy springs from that moment of mutual recognition when the Indians turned him out into the wilderness with the body of Amalie. In that moment a "mark" was fixed on Clement. "There is nothing that you can see," he tells Jamie, "but something came out of their eyes." Clement cannot say what his mark means; but he does share, in an intuitive way, the Indians' strange and doomed relationship with time. He says, "They are sure of the future growing smaller always . . . ." The future is also dwindling for the two men, the robber and the planter, as they sit and talk in the Rodney tavern, for the town itself will eventually be removed from the mainstream of human commerce.

Although the Indians and the town of Rodney may be seen as symbols for limited time, extinction, or the vanity of human pride and industry, they are never explicitly tapped and identified by the author as her symbols. Miss Welty uses place and its spirit more subtly, trusting it to generate its own symbolic meaning in its own time. She writes that "place in fiction is the named, identified, concrete, exact and exacting, and therefore credible, gathering-spot of all that has been felt, is about to be experienced, in the novel's progress."[10] The extinction of the Natchez and the eventual death of Rodney are always both finished facts "about to be experienced"; they haunt the

10. Eudora Welty, "Place in Fiction," *The South Atlantic Quarterly*, 55 (January 1956), 62.

place of this novel. Miss Welty's choices here are essential to the meaning of *The Robber Bridegroom* and for the right appreciation of her technique. The historical details in her novel are not what Chester Eisinger has called "an act of harmless piety,"[11] but are rather a vital creative act.

With the passing of the Indians, an intimate human connection with the natural world passes too. They are so closely united with the world of animals and forest that disguise, as Clement can testify, is as natural to them as skin. Hidden and beyond the lights and noise of the artificial world of the pioneers, the Indians are always watching, ready to proclaim a "reckoning." When the second and climactic reckoning falls due, the Indians materialize and apprehend the white offenders as if they [the Indians] were the avenging shapes of the forest itself. The bush at Salome's side "comes alive," and she is taken. A "red hand" materializes in an apparently empty forest, and Clement is taken. An Indian "appeared suddenly before [Rosamond] in the mask of a spotty leopard," and she is carried off.

The Indians seize their captives to avenge the rape and desecration of their people, symbolically committed when Little Harp, the vicious killer of the Natchez Trace who is based on an historical figure, violates and kills an innocent Indian girl while Jamie's robber cohorts cheer. This violation scene is a departure from the fantasy of the fairy tale, and a vivid example of the violence that threads through the story as local legend. There is no irony in the scene. On a table littered with the leavings of a meal, Little Harp first

---

11. Chester Eisinger, *Fiction of the Forties* (Chicago: University of Chicago Press, 1965), p. 273.

cuts off the drugged girl's finger, then throws himself upon her. When he leaves her, she is dead; no magic wand can revive her. A new and brutal power has entered the realm of the "pacific" Natchez. The power is the power of greed, and everyone is infected.

Jamie Lockhart, whose sole interest is the accumulation of capital, is the dashing hero of this new time—"Take first and ask afterward" is our hero's motto. Rosamond, damsel that she appears to be, becomes Jamie's wife and then the mistress of a mansion more lavish than the one her wicked stepmother coveted. And Salome herself is the perfect essence of exploitation and greed: ". . . we must cut down more of the forest, and stretch away the fields until we grow twice as much cotton, twice as much tobacco. For the land is there for the taking, and I say, take it." [12] It is little wonder that the Indians of history and of fiction, faced with this plague of locusts, react with violence to defend themselves, but are overcome.

The second reckoning of the novel is the Indians' twilight; they appear weary and decimated, faint shadows of their former, "blazing" selves. They have been exhausted in the struggle against the intruders; for them "sleep had come to be sweeter than revenge." Salome insults the sun, the Indians' divinity, and they hesitate to strike her dead. In former times she would have been exe-

---

12. The similarity between the relationship of Salome and Clement, and Adam and the Eve of Progress in John Crowe Ransom's essay "Reconstructed but Unregenerate" (*I'll Take My Stand* [New York: Harper Torchbooks, 1962]) is striking; it supports the view that *The Robber Bridegroom* devotes at least one facet to cultural comment. In Ransom's essay Adam resists Eve's Progressivism and prodding. The function of Eve in industrial society, Ransom says, is "the seducing of laggard men into fresh struggles with nature" (p. 10).

cuted on the spot. And the recognition of a broader meaning in the doomed Indians is left to Clement.

And Clement, from where he was bound, saw the sad faces of the Indians, like the faces of feverish children, and said to himself, "The savages have only come the sooner to their end; we will come to ours too. Why have I built my house, and added to it? The planter will go after the hunter, and the merchant after the planter, all having their day."

Clement sees, in the faces of the Indians, the inescapable human fate of extinction. They are, to him, just another group of human beings overtaken by change, as he himself will be overtaken. He is the planter about to give place to the merchant, Jamie. A stronger, more brutally efficient force is always wresting control of the present. The Indians, and, increasingly, Clement are relics of the past.

Clement Musgrove is a character in a cast of caricatures. To borrow E. M. Forster's terms, he is "round" while the others are "flat." The pioneer cast includes the stereotypical hero, damsel, and the wicked stepmother, but Clement is a person of considerable dimension and depth. He enters the novel with the naive innocence of Don Quixote or Candide, but he grows, through the development of his conscience, memory, and sympathy, toward an encompassing vision. Like the Indians, he is pushed aside by time and change. Like the Indians also, he is overtaken by and must come to terms with history.

While the pioneers around him are ruthlessly taking everything that is not nailed down, Clement cannot, or will not, push himself over the psychological threshold that bars him from adding to his possessions. His conscience is the barrier. Salome's insistent greed dismays him: "'To encompass so much as that is greedy. . . . It would take too much of time and the heart's energy." Ownership, for Clement, is a matter of conscience; it is more emotionally complex than the mere piling up of land or loot. But, such is the malleable condition of his conscience, as it grows, that he bends to Salome's desire and adds to his plantation, hoping, with a fair amount of self-delusion, that each new demand will be her last.

The toll of pioneering into the wilderness is collected from Clement's heart. The Indians were cleared away along with the trees of the forest; the guilt of that offense lodges in Clement. While the Indians and the forest were outright victims of pioneering, Clement is a victim in a more complicated way. He carries the burden of guilt, and the more he sees, the heavier the burden becomes.

There is no mistaking the quality of naive vulnerability in Clement when he appears. He steps from the riverboat into the flush times of Rodney carrying, in plain sight, "a bag of gold and many presents." His riches are protected with nothing more formidable than his own "tight grip," although the place is swarming with bandits. We also learn that Clement has sold his tobacco for a "fair price." In flush times there were fortunes to be made. But Clement is not a tycoon, not a wheeler-dealer, and not, apparently, motivated by the desire for great profit. He lives up to his name: he is a fair, "clement" man, avoiding extremes of profit and poverty. But the world in which he lives is, on the contrary, a world of wild extremes. And, as if to underline the contrast between Clement's "clemency" and the wide-open world of the frontier, a fabulous storm whirls into Rodney minutes after Clement debarks.

There is another facet to Clement's guilessness: his gullibility. Rejecting the deceit and deviousness in plain sight (a series of innkeepers whose missing ears signify punishment for their past crimes), Clement is duped by dishonesty that he fails to see. When at last he meets an innkeeper with both ears intact, he fails to notice how those ears perk up like a rabbit's at the tempting prospect of such a rich and unsuspecting customer as himself. Clement, to his grief, pronounces this innkeeper an honest man.

A shrewder and more worldly person would not automatically accept people at face value; he would have the imagination of evil to suspect duplicity. But Clement's imagination is, as yet, innocent of such things. He prefers the illusion of his worldly wisdom to a real and vigilant skepticism. In choosing Jamie Lockhart to hear his life history, Clement is again guided by "face value"; to him Jamie "was remarkably amiable to see. But by his look, nobody could tell what he would do". Not surprisingly, Jamie entirely misses the import of Clement's story. He listens with the face of a gentleman, but also with the ears of a bandit, all the time calculating how much Clement might be worth.

Clement's story shows the signs of a heart that feels the costs of pioneering, in sorrow, loss, general estrangement, and of a mind that is beginning to be puzzled about the reasons. There has been a great enduring separation in Clement's life. He prefaces his history with

The reason I ever came is forgotten now. . . . I know I am not a seeker after anything and ambition in this world never stirred my heart once. Yet it seemed as if I was caught up by what came over the others, and they were the same. There was a great tug at the whole world, to go down over the edge, and one and all we were changed into pioneers, and our hearts and our lonely wills may have had nothing to do with it.

After the separation came the homelessness of the dis-
placed person, and Clement, without ambition, without
the motivation to seek, to pile up, is an alien in the pioneer
life.

At first Clement is only aware of the pain of dislocation,
not of its causes. His memory preserves the name of
former comfort and peace: Amalie. Her name suggests a
natural kinship with Clement, but she is also part of the
past that Clement has left behind. The temptation to "go
home again" is as strong as the memory itself. Clement
confesses to Jamie that he often struggles in a dream with
the tensions he keeps down while awake: "In the dream,
whenever I lie down, then it is the past. When I climb to
my feet, then it is the present. And I keep up a struggle not
to fall."

Clement is moored to the past, like the town of Rodney
and the Indians. But, unlike them both, he is tied to a long
line, human history, that casts him into the future. This is
an unusual and complicated situation for a character in a
mere "simple" fairy tale. Time is not a real consideration
for Mike Fink, for Jamie Lockhart, or for Rosamond. But
Clement is part of the author's concern with change. He is
the only character in the novel capable of appreciating,
perhaps not intellectually from the beginning, but surely
intuitively, the expanse of time that will eventually erase
all human enterprise. Everyone else is wrapped up in the
here and now, unable or unwilling to appreciate the present as a single moment in a constant flow from the past
toward the future.

Jamie Lockhart, from his limited perspective, is full of
advice for Clement. When the going gets deep and heavy,
Jamie counsels that one should discard all the useless
moral baggage. Here are two proverbs from simple Jamie:

"Don't fret over the reason, for it may have been in the stars."

"Guilt is a burdensome thing to carry about in the heart. I would never bother with it."

Clement recognizes the advice; he answers Jamie: "Then you are a man of action . . . a man of the times, a pioneer and a free agent. There is no one to come to you saying 'I want' what you do not want . . . ."

For Jamie and his fellow pioneers, the chance to grab the wealth of a lifetime in one stroke—the main chance—is too great to be complicated by intangibles like conscience, morality, or the heart. The main chance is the irresistible "tug" that has drawn the pioneers, and continues to draw them, through acts of greed and violence, toward the material goal. Clement knows better than anyone, being married to Salome, how strong is the temptation to take, to exploit, to own what no one—no white man—has possessed before. Back in civilization there were norms and customs and laws to check such unruly impulses as greed and grandiose schemes of personal possession. But those checks did not follow the pioneers into the wilderness. The lack of them creates a moral wilderness that baffles Clement as much as the natural one does. In such a world, he thinks it better to conserve life's energy rather than to risk it for loot that, besides being ephemeral, collects a tax from the human heart.

For the pioneer, the past is left behind, that segment of history is put away. But Clement's memory of the past is the keystone of his character. As he recalls the little group of white men and women huddled around a campfire just before the Indians effortlessly penetrated the circle and shattered the illusion of security, he is reminded that nothing he gathers around himself for familiarity and protection is as formidable, as impenetrable, as it seems. In time Clement learns that even his own "family circle" (Salome, Jamie, Rosamond) is vulnerable. They leave him alone, each one pursuing his or her own dreams of wealth and success. Clement lives in his heart, and the heart's time is not history but myth—the pastoral. He has seen in the faces of the Indians pride and triumph brought down to impotence and weariness as their time runs out. And he accepts himself as an "end" and Jamie as a "beginning" in the constant process of time.

But "he was an innocent of the wilderness . . . and this was his good." It is essential to his innocence that he remain "clement," shunning extremes and leaving action of violent resistance to the Indians to the Salomes and Jamies. His way is contemplation.

Finally, in his moment of private reckoning, Clement sees each individual tree and bird, and also the continuity of all things. Time bothers him most persistently ("What is the place and time?"). The trees grow straight and tall, and birds sing from the branches. Everything seems to be harmonious and ordered, but there is a menacing presence that threatens the tranquility:

. . . and across this floor, slowly and softly and forever moving into profile, is always a beast, one of the procession, weighted low with his burning coat, looking from the yellow eye set in his head.

A beast like that of impending chaos in Yeats' "The Second Coming" haunts Clement's vision. He worries, like Yeats, that the way of the world is down from order, accelerating toward chaos, that history is not building and making but, ironically, is man's demolition of the original, pastoral integrity of creation.

Clement's thoughts and emotions in his moment of choice are complex; he is deeply troubled by a sense of the contradictions in things and people. The mutability of all things haunts his consciousness, yet all around him he sees people living in ignorance of it. Clement's personal outlook, in this respect, is a more conscious and reflective version of the outlook of the Indians. His special relationship with them is not gratuitous. He knows what they only feel: their inescapable doom in the waves of white pioneers. And he knows something further: that the "tug" pulling the pioneers will result in nothing more permanent than the life the Indians had. Rodney is the place to verify that.

Two worlds clash, in Clement's vision, and the old will be destroyed. The beast with the single yellow eye is the harbinger of the new, forever revolving into the present. The beast means for Clement that the end point of progress is not a perfect pastoral Eden on earth. How can that be the culmination, Clement must think, even though the dreams and hopes and images luring the pioneers are the most desirable the human imagination can create? How can this pioneering adventure end in idyll when it is based on "doubleness," on greed that is called a noble errand, on ambition that shuts out every human consideration except the piling up of fantastic gain? He laments:

"But the time for cunning has come . . . And my time is over, for cunning is of a world I will have no part in. Two long ripples are following down the Mississippi behind the approaching somnolent eyes of the alligator. And like the tenderest deer, a band of copying Indians poses along the bluff to draw us near them. Men are following men down the Mississippi, hoarse and arrogant by day, wakeful and dreamless by night at the unknown landings. A trail leads like a tunnel under the roof of this wilderness.

Everywhere the traps are set. Why? And what kind of time is this, when all is first given, then stolen away?"

Just as all pursuers of the pastoral attend the romantic dream of earthly perfection, until the means of getting it prove invalid and false, Clement Musgrove follows the pioneer trail until, in time, he learns the cost to the human heart. To continue to pursue, he would have had to assume a "doubleness" toward himself and the world, taking what was there and pretending it was free.

The Robber Bridegroom, then, in juxtaposing pastoral and history, fairy tale and reality, achieves something more than simplicity, as Mr. Trilling thought, and more than harmless piety or even a happy ending, as Mr. Eisinger has written. By looking away from the zany goings-on, by concentrating on Clement and the Indians, one can see very clearly the somber current of a theme that completes the humor, that makes the whole greater than its parts, but that really should not be talked about separate from the humor. The artist can do more than the critic, though; she can say these two things at once.

Woman's World, Man's Place:
The Fiction of Eudora Welty

PEGGY W. PRENSHAW

WHEN I WAS A LITTLE GIRL growing up
in a little Mississippi town in the 1940s, my days were
spent mostly in a pleasurable routine of family, school, and
play, which was almost always "p'like." What my friends
and I played like, of course, was being grown up, being
alluring, beautiful women, brides, mothers with husbands and children to command. In our imagined house-
holds, desires were swiftly answered with simple will—
dreams of love came true with a pretended lover or baby.

As I grew into adolescence, I lived the life of the imagination less and less with dolls and playmates, more with
the books in the one-room library that offered a world, as
Eudora Welty has said, for a sweet devouring. When I was
nine or ten, I remember the librarian's urging on me a new
book by a Mississippi writer. It had all the things I liked
best, she said—a motherless girl who found a new family,
young lovers, a wedding, and a haunted house. And so I
took it along with the one other I was allowed at the twice
weekly opening of the library.

Delta Wedding was not at all what I expected, or
wanted. Though I don't remember the other book, I am

46

sure I read it first and only grudgingly went on with the strange, unexciting book that lacked so much of what I favored. The bridegroom wasn't handsome, the ceremony wasn't romantic, and the haunted house wasn't scary. It was not a girl's book. Not until later, after I had married and returned to college, did I come again to read Eudora Welty's fiction. But the stories had waited for me, and, reading them with some knowledge of the heart as well as desire, I found a world I vaguely recognized. It lacked the simple romance of a girl's dreams, but it shone forth in a reflection of mystery and everydayness, love and uncertainty that I had begun to see as my world—and to think about.

Through the years I have come to comprehend my terrain more surely, to a considerable degree because Miss Welty has shown me how to open my eyes to see. But focusing now on her fictional world, I feel somewhat uncertain of the boundary between my perceiving and the stories' showing. Teacher that I am, ordinarily I duck the old ontological problem and proclaim myself the ideal reader Cleanth Brooks has tried to teach us how to be. Now, however, an admission of wariness seems in order, for I am anxious about the topography I have mapped here, about the announcement that Miss Welty's fiction reveals a woman's world. It sounds distinctly like the report of a new feminist critic, but perhaps that is what I am.

Eudora Welty reveals a world brimming with life— natural, sensual, rational, moral—and she invests in her characters, male and female, a boundless capacity for bodying forth the rich diversity. They bid for attention and praise when, wisely, like old Phoenix Jackson, they shape their lives in obedience to the ancient laws of birth and death or when, heroically, like Julia Mortimer, they pursue a private vision.

As Simone de Beauvoir has shown, we are accustomed to thinking of these two human destinies as characteristically sexual.[1] Traditionally, the woman's place is in the home. She is the mother who gives us life and with it our mortality. Transcendence of death comes from her in nature's promise of natural renewal, a sexual immortality. By contrast, man justifies his being in vaunting, death-defying acts of courage. He redeems the natural life by winning significance for the separate person and the single moment. Throughout most of Western civilization, his daring in the face of death has led to a tragic grandeur more admirable and uplifting than comedies of renewal. But such conventions are not the way of Welty's world, in which heroes are more often female than male and, regardless of sex, possess a grandeur that ultimately pales in the cycles of nature's, and the family's, renewing life. Take *Delta Wedding*, which presents a grandly matriarchal order, the ancient order of powerful mothers. Nine-year-old Laura McRaven leaves Jackson and her widowed father to attend the wedding of cousin Dabney Fairchild. The return to Shellmound Plantation in many ways represents for Laura a recovery of her mother, for the Fairchilds are her mother's clan and the plantation is the place of Laura's birth. Despite her longing to join the family circle, to be a member of the wedding, she is at times nearly overwhelmed by the thriving, heedless life of the eight cousins, and the ordered, measured control of the aunts and great-aunts. It occurs to her that "when people were at

1. *The Second Sex*, trans. H. M. Parshley (1953; rpt. New York: Vintage-Random House, 1974), pp. 71–74.

Shellmound it was as if they had never been anywhere else." In fact, Laura thinks of the plantation as the center of life:

> . . . it was as if they considered her mother all the time as belonging, in her life and in her death (for they took Laura and *let* her see the grave), as belonging here; they considered Shellmound the important part of life and death too. All they remembered and told her about was likely to be before Laura was born, and they could say so easily, "Before—or after—Annie Laurie died . . . ," to count the time of a dress being made or a fruit tree planted.

Death at Shellmound contains few horrors, so easily does it yield to the assurance of nature's repeating cycles. In the scene in which Laura in the cemetery struggles against the memory of her mother, she and the cousins run into Dr. Murdoch, the family physician. The exchange illustrates clearly the source of Fairchild power. "He tipped his hat to Shelley, and then puckering his handsome, pale lips, looked down at the Fairchild graves. 'How many more of you are there?' he said suddenly." Shelley, the oldest, answers quickly, but then, clearly caught off guard, admits she has forgot the old people and even the little Jackson cousin standing beside her. No matter, Dr. Murdoch obviously is calculating numbers loosely anyway. What engages him is the broad solid line of the family stretching from its graves into its future. "Dabney and that fellow she's marrying will have three or four at the least. That will give them room, over against the Hunters. . . . Primrose and Jim Allen naturally go here, in line with Rowena and What's-his-name that was killed, and his wife. An easy two here. George and the Reid girl probably won't have children—he doesn't strike me as a family man." The *memento mori* loses its traditional somberness not just through the doctor's teasing, good-natured brusqueness, but from the incontrovertible fact that the graveyard will hardly contain the present generations, much less the boundless Fairchild families of the future. When he begins to consider their progeny—Shelley will probably have a houseful like her mother, he says—he finally gives up his assignment of grave sites: "How many more of you are there? I've lost track."

Not only does the matriarchal order express itself in the human and natural fertility of Shellmound, but in the busy activity of the plantation. Everywhere one encounters the work and ceremonies of women in an agrarian society. Cooking and feeding occupy much of their time. Ellen draws Laura into the comfort of the family by letting her help bake a "Mashula Hines" cake. Jim Allen and Primrose are distinguished by their complementary talents— one the cake maker, the other a specialist in preserving and candy making. Typically the loving, nurturing side of the Fairchilds shows up in their gifts of food. Laden plates go out and return magically laden with different foods. As the children know well, for they are the errand-runners, one never sends back an empty plate. Even the prestige of the family is gauged by the quantity and quality of the table it sets. Ellen worries not only about Dabney's future happiness but about the wedding food: "Now I'm thinking about the chicken salad—we've made two or three tubs and got it covered in ice—and do you think frozen tomato salad turned in the freezer would be a reproach on us for the rehearsal supper?"

The cooking, sewing, gardening—the nurturing—are not trivial activities, or, if they are, the way of life is trivial, for its ways and values are formed in these rhythms of work. Beautiful handmade quilts of treasured patterns—like Delectable Mountains—go out to newlyweds to help in the making of the new home. A handmade stocking doll holds Laura's most vivid memory of her mother's love. The account of the dollmaking, in fact, embodies the significance of the Shellmound culture. One hot, humid summer afternoon, having just returned to Jackson from a visit to the plantation, Laura's mother offers to make a doll. While her father stands in the hallway winding the clock—he always likes to know what time it is—Laura and her mother go to the sewing baskets, finding the scraps and pieces that lead irresistibly to the new creation. The heightened tone of the prose suggests the drama of childbirth. Wearing a blue dress, her hair disheveled from the car ride, Laura's mother is "excited, smiling, young—as the cousins were always, but as she was not always—for the air at Shellmound was pleasure and excitement, pleasure that did not need to be explained, tears that could go a nice long time unsilenced, and the air of Jackson was different." While under the spell of the Delta, racing to finish the doll before a threatening storm breaks outside, she makes Laura a baby named Marmion, named for one of the Fairchild plantation houses near Shellmound. The great empty house is Annie Laurie's inheritance and will one day perhaps be Laura's. As her Uncle Battle says, "Someday you'll live there like your Aunt Ellen here, with all your children." The gesture of Annie Laurie's handing the doll to her daughter, an act of a loving mother, prideful of her skills, is the generational correlative of "passing the torch" in Julia Mortimer's realm in *Losing Battles*. The mother's link forms the human chain, and in *Delta Wedding* the connections lead ultimately, even mystically, back to the earth.

In a passage reflecting the consciousness of the outsider Robbie Reid, the connection between the women and the land is bluntly stated: "It was notoriously the women of the Fairchilds who since the Civil War, or—who knew?—since the Indian times, ran the household and had everything at their fingertips—not the men. The women it was who inherited the place—or their brothers, guiltily, handed it over." Robbie sees that "in the Delta the land belonged to the women—they only let the men have it, and sometimes they tried to take it back and give it to someone else." Poor landless girl in love with Memphis, Robbie is at a loss to understand either the land transactions or the Fairchild women's oblique command of power. But she recognizes it as the power Elizabeth Janeway describes in *Man's World, Woman's Place* as the dominance of the givers, whose riches and substance are needed and thus bestowed upon children and men. Robbie thinks, "It was as if the women had exacted the place, the land, for something—for something they had had to give. Then, so as to be all gracious and noble, they had let it out of their hands—with a play of the reins—to the men. . . ."

The family pattern that we see here resembles the ancient agricultural communities Simone de Beauvoir describes in *The Second Sex.* She writes of the early nomads, who were followed by clans attached to the soil; these were cultivators who established a unity and identity with the land they worked, land that required a posterity to inherit it and assure the clan's permanence:

In place of the outlook of the nomadic tribes, living only for the moment, the agricultural community substituted the concept of a life rooted in the past and connected with the future. . . . the clan took a profound interest in its own descendants, for it would achieve survival through the land that it would bequeath to them and that they would exploit. The community sensed its unity and desired a continued existence beyond the present; it recognized itself in its children, recognized them as its own; and in them it found fulfillment and transcendence.

Beauvoir goes on to speak of the role of the mother in this primitive society, a role of enormous prestige because the woman was so obviously necessary for the birth of the child:

Very often the children belonged to their mother's clan, carried its name, and shared its rights and privileges, particularly in the use of the land held by the clan. Communal property was handed down by the women: through them ownership in the fields and harvests was assured to members of the clan, and conversely these members were destined through their mothers for this or that domain. We may suppose, then, that in a mystical sense the earth belonged to the women: they had a hold, at once religious and legal, upon the land and its fruits. The tie between woman and land was still closer than that of ownership, for the matrilineal regime was characterized by a veritable assimilation of woman to the earth; in both the permanence of life—which is essentially generation—was accomplished through the reproduction of its individual embodiments, its avatars.[2]

Delta Wedding, set in 1923, gives us a world rooted in this ancient past. Miss Welty said once in an interview that in planning the novel she made "a careful investigation to find the year in which nothing very terrible had happened in the Delta by way of floods or fires or wars which would have taken the men away."[3] Battle and George Fairchild

---

2. *The Second Sex*, pp. 75–76.

3. Linda Kuehle, "The Art of Fiction XLVII: Eudora Welty," *Paris Review*, 55 (Fall 1972), 85.

and bridegroom Troy Flavin are, to be sure, present throughout the action of the novel, but their role—their place—is chiefly defined by their relationship to the women. Let me be clear about what I find distinctive here. The Fairchild women are neither more nor less *domineering* than the women one finds typically in a nineteenth-century plantation novel, or a Faulkner novel, or in actual experience. But their functions and rituals *dominate* the action of the novel and signify its vital impulse—the joyous celebration of the green and dying life that is the earthly province of women.

In *Delta Wedding* the cycle of ever-renewing natural life attaches to the fertile land and to the female Fairchilds. Ellen is pregnant with her ninth child; cousin Mary Denis Summers Buchanan has just given birth; daughter Bluet is the rosy-cheeked baby of the clan. The nine-year-olds—Maureen, Lady Clare, India, and especially Laura—all stand on the child's side of puberty, intrigued by the grownup world and caught up by the excitement of Dabney's wedding, a ritual that awes older sister Shelley. Like Cassie Morrison of "June Recital," Shelley desires and fears the passionate sacrifice of the self that the wedding signifies. By contrast, Dabney pursues marriage with the same relish and sense of celebration that Roxie, Vi'let and Little Uncle show in announcing young Pinchy's entry into the ranks of womanhood. The aunts, Primrose and Jim Allen, for all their maidenhood, are not so much sterile as virginal keepers of the family's stories and patterns and recipes—the revered ways of the past, which like the land are passed on to succeeding generations of Fairchilds. Childless, they are nevertheless mothers like Great-Aunts Mac and Shannon, who reared the seven Fairchild nieces and nephews. They serve to teach the human bond, particularly the obligation of the men to nurture the women and children. In her book *Male and Female*, Margaret Mead discusses human fatherhood as a "social invention," noting that the basic biological unit is mother and child while the basic unit of human society is the family, which rests upon the learned nurturing behavior of men. Such behavior, she writes, is tenuous and fragile and can disappear rather easily under social conditions that do not teach it effectively.[4] That Battle and George are well taught offers testimony of the success of their aunts' and sisters' mothering.

To a degree sister Tempe stands outside the steady, timeless life of the plantation. Like Annie Laurie she married and moved to the town, and she regards Shellmound as shamefully permissive and old fashioned. She resembles Lizzie Stark in *The Golden Apples* or Becky McKelva in *The Optimist's Daughter*, who resist an easy acquiescence to life's disorderly ways. But drawn into the circle of Shellmound life, Tempe can no more hold out against it than she can resist red-haired Mr. Buchanan's claim of her daughter—or red-haired Troy Flavin's claim of Dabney. Resigned, she too acquiesces to Fairchild life. At the wedding rehearsal, young Ranny weaves through the group shouting, "I'm the wedding!" Herald of the renewing life of the clan, green peach limb in hand, he at last runs to Aunt Tempe, shouting still as he twirls her about, and "in that moment Tempe, laughing, experienced not a thought exactly but a truer thing, a suspicion, that what she loved was not gone with Denis [the dead brother], but was, perhaps, perennial. . . . Indeed the Fairchilds took you in cirles, whirring delightedly about, she thought,

---

4. *Male and Female* (1949; rpt. New York: Mentor, 1962), pp. 146–48.

stirring up confusions, hopefully working themselves up."

Even the aged black women have their place in the circle of Shellmound. Particularly interesting is Aunt Studney, "coal-black, old as the hills, with her foot always in the road." She appears, like an ancient goddess, to assure rebirth and renewal. She is like the crone of Walt Whitman's poem, endlessly rocking the cradle, or like the phoenix who encloses within itself the miracle of death and birth. On the day that Laura and Roy slip away to the Yazoo River, the river of death, and cross over to Marmion, for many years an empty house of death, they encounter Aunt Studney with her mysterious sack—where babies come from, Roy thinks. Old Aunt Studney, whose single phrase is "Ain't studyin' you," arrives as if ceremoniously to bestow life on the house that Dabney and Troy will occupy. When the children enter Marmion, they find dead birds everywhere, lying on their sides, like people. The vast seductive house with closed doors opens almost erotically to their searching, curious exploration. As they run through the house of life and death, Aunt Studney's ritualistic dance comes as ordained and ordinary. She "stood holding her sack on the floor between her feet with her hands knotted together over its mouth. . . . She did not move at all except to turn herself in place around and around, arms bent and hovering, like an old bird over her one egg." The cry she makes, high and threatening, sounds like the "first note of a song at a ceremony, a wedding or a funeral, and like the bark of a dog too, somehow." It is like the "harsh, human sounds" described at the conclusion of "At the Landing" when Jenny Lockhart's cry mingles with the fisherman's rude laugh, in what sounds ambiguously like rejoicing.

As if all the pains and pleasures of the world have escaped from Aunt Studney's sack, Marmion suddenly comes to life. Bees fly out everywhere, startling Laura with a dizzying excitement. The whole episode is rich with details of psychological passage, as Laura and Roy journey from the protection of Shellmound to the ominous Marmion, to the encounter with the old woman and sack, to an eventual immersion in the river of death. But I should like to concentrate here on Aunt Studney's presence.

Both she and Partheny, who is often "mindless" but is revered for her gift of second sight, her intuition, appear as keepers of the women's mysteries. As the white aunts inculcate the mysteries of the women's crafts and nurturing skills, so the black aunts instruct in the sexual mysteries. Studney's sack, like Pandora's box, holds the mystery of childbirth and female sexuality. Partheny's house, set deeply in shaded Brunswick-town amid figs and flowers, hens and pigeons, has an eerie female presence. Strange smells mix with "smells of darkness," in the words of the novel. The earth beneath the house is bare like feet; the door opens like an eye behind a veil; stovepipes crook like elbows. Partheny, high priestess of erotic love, mixes a charmed patticake whose magic is supposed to return Robbie to George's bed. And when the time comes finally for the Delta wedding, Partheny arrives to dress Dabney, dismissing Roxie and the virginal Shelley and Aunt Primrose with a "Git out, Nothin'."

To the child Laura, on the verge of adolescence, the pre-eminent mentors and models are female. She apprehends a Fairchild world that is archetypally natural and feminine. In this world the women range in type from the active motherly to the erotically feminine, to use the

language of Helen Deutsch in *The Psychology of Women*.[5]
Motherly managers like Tempe, Jim Allen, and Mac pride
themselves on their self-sufficiency and take over the direction of men and children as a natural right and duty.
Their type recurs frequently in Miss Welty's fiction. Lizzie
Morgan Stark of *Golden Apples* tries to regulate the society of Morgana, but, playing Hera to King McLain's Zeus
of Morgan's Woods, she manages at best to be Snowdie's
defender and Camp Mother of the "Moon Lake" girls. The
lady friends of Lily Daw, Mrs. Marblehall, Sabina McInnis
of "Asphodel," all defenders of the feminine faith, guard
against masculine fickleness and desertion of duty to
women and children. They protect human society by im-
posing sanctions and restraints meant to fortify the family.

For all their active bossiness, however, these women are
family-centered and do not seek a separate life. In one extraordinary novel, *The Ponder Heart*, Miss Welty has
shown us how it feels to be such a woman, what the world
looks like from the inside of a cherished and locked family
circle. Edna Earle Ponder mothers Grandfather and Uncle
Daniel, trying to guard against the consequences of the
Ponder heart. But Bonnie Dee Peacock, like Wanda Fay of
The Optimist's Daughter, appears as predictably as a jay-
bird or the weather, threatening the continuity of the
family with her erotic and careless femininity. In one respect, however, Edna Earle and Bonnie Dee resemble one
another—in the almost total absence of doubt and am-
biguity in their world. One is sure of purpose, the other
purposeless. Both belong to the natural, perennial life of a
matriarchal society, the realm of earth goddess Demeter,

---

5. *The Psychology of Women* (1944; rpt. New York: Bantam, 1973), I,
286 ff.

who gives the periodicity of seasons, the nourishing grain, the protected hearth, and the sign of rebirth in the recovery of a beloved daughter. Again, in a story like "Ladies in Spring," when Hattie Purcell marches into the woods, black hatted, with long furled umbrella in hand, everyone understands she intends to bring rain to the dry countryside. Preoccupied with her main business, she casually, almost incidentally, rounds up wandering husbands, truant schoolboys, and misplaced nieces in the course of her journey. In one movement she bestows fertility to the land and thwarts illicit lovemaking. She is goddess of all she surveys, postmistress as well as rainmaker, and her mediation between the outside world and the world of Royals is calculated and controlled, for "Miss Hattie never let her powers interfere with mail time, or mail time interfere with her powers. She had everything worked out."

Many other female characters in Miss Welty's fiction belong to this great interrelated human family that takes joy in an assured, unself-conscious life. Less designing and assertive than the Edna Earles and Hatties are several of the aged mothers, who are wise and nurturing, like "code heroes" drawing instinctively from the wellspring of life. Phoenix Jackson and Nonna, the grandmother in "Going to Naples," seem always to have known that the essence of life is love—the caring touch, the earthly bond. "The human voice alone is divine," says Nonna.

Although not so quietly grand, the noisy Fairchilds and the Beecham clan of *Losing Battles* live for love and each other, not for thought and abstract principle. And the Peacocks, Dalzells, and Chisoms, happily self-preoccupied, finally expose the limits of a wholly shared and insensible life. They seem to emerge from an earlier age, one that predates the origins of consciousness, and answer to compulsions and needs unambiguously perceived. Theirs is a mentality related to what Julian Jaynes describes in his recent study of the origin of consciousness.[6] They live in a state of unconsciousness like that existing in ancient civilizations, which produced human action—immediate and certain—without feeling or thought.

The range of the woman's world I have described is vast; it derives from a matriarchal principle that extends from the sensual, instinctual realm, which, to use a classical analogue, we may associate with Aphrodite and Eros, to the ordering, protecting, domestic realm of a Hera. And both aspects are contained in the mythic Great Mother—a Gaea or Demeter who rules the natural fertile world, presiding over birth and death of the vegetable and animal species, oblivious to separate human psyches. In his analysis of the Psyche myth, Erich Neumann has in fact described this Great Mother as the feminine archetype of the unconscious, and the relationship of mother and daughter—the myth of Demeter and Persephone—as the primordial feminine relation.[7]

The world of the mothers, whether viewed as a reflection of matriarchal bonds tracing from the ancient past or a psychological representation of the unconscious, is a world wrapped in a cocoon of sufficiency, needing little of men and less of the vaunting, heroic gestures that we think of as the masculine task of facing and slaying the dragon. Rather, the men are desired and needed for their

---

6. *The Origins of Consciousness in the Breakdown of the Bicameral Mind* (Boston: Houghton Mifflin, 1976).

7. *Amor and Psyche,* trans. Ralph Manheim (1956; rpt. New York: Harper Torchbooks, 1962), p. 131.

potency, their power to inseminate and revitalize the static feminine world. Promiscuous, wild, Dionysiac, they prance on the scene, bedazzling a country girl like Livvie, horrifying a battle axe like Lizzie Stark, but they are recognized and accepted by both as a needed life giver. In "Livvie," Cash McCord, in leaf-green Easter coat and with guinea pig in pocket, enters the ordered, sterile house, stamping, flinging his head, making a noise like a hoof pawing the floor. For all the cost to Solomon's design and artistry, Cash's arrival returns Livvie to the land of mothers and children.

Similarly, Don McInnis in "Asphodel" appears on his wedding night as a roaring Pan, turning his head like an animal, trampling the scattered flowers. Unlike Livvie, imperious Sabina despises the beast who is her husband. She is unreconciled to his fateful attractiveness and his irreverent, careless regard for women and children, but she nonetheless admits him to her bed because he will father her children. In this regard, Bruno Bettelheim in analyzing the animal groom of fairy tales, discusses the marriage to the beast as a symbolic stage of an immature fear and loathing of sexuality, and the transformation of the beast as the selfless and conscious act of a mature love.[8] That Miss Sabina does not "transform the beast" suggests her failure to reach beyond the complacent, matriarchal world to sympathetic, conscious feeling. In fact, in looking at Livvie and Sabina we see that whether the lover is accepted as a natural sexual partner or grudgingly endured as a needed inseminator, the relationships are similarly devoid of a humanizing *consciousness*. So it is with characters in other stories. Snowdie Hudson blinks hap-

---

8. *The Uses of Enchantment* (New York: Knopf, 1976), pp. 278–79.

pily when King McLain descends in a shower of gold, but as Katie Rainey says, she never "got a real good look at life." Lizzie Stark is outraged but finally endures Loch Morrison's presence astraddle Easter, his urgent lifesaving motion to force life upon her. Half-witted Lily Daw takes a red-headed xylophone player instead of a trip to Ellisville; pregnant wives Marjorie in "Flowers for Marjorie" and Sonny's wife in "Death of a Traveling Salesman" accept their world with magical ease, having nothing to prove or conquer, nothing to *see*. For the most part, the husbands and lovers, like summer kings or field gods, perform a role like the one the "Moon Lake" girls ascribe to Loch Morrison: a "silly, brief, overriding little show . . . there in his tent of separation in the middle of the woods, in the night." Life for Cash, or Billy Floyd of "At the Landing," is, as for King, a "blithe, smiling, superior, frantic existence," a life, one might say, without conscious love.

Of course, some of the wives and mothers-to-be like William Wallace Jamison's Hazel or Jamie Lockhart's Rosamond, teach their wild boyish lovers about the complexity of love, and like the mythic Pysche they transform them into husbands, fathers, who are rescued first from naive innocence and then from threatening loneliness. At the conclusion of "The Wide Net," Hazel takes William Wallace by the hand and leads him into the house, "smiling as if she were smiling down on him."

Whenever conscious separation from the maternal, domestic circle does come to a character, it brings distress, especially for the males. Often they are unable to cope with the separateness and search for reunion with the mother—or wife. Ron and Eugene McLain long for a father's direction to show them how to cure their loneliness, but significantly it is Snowdie whom Ron addresses in his pained internal dialogue. The separation from her brought his original terror and the return to Jenny his eventual solace. "The Lord never meant us all to separate," he says. One day in San Francisco Eugene awakens to the emptiness of his life with Emma, but after a day-long epic quest, he comes at last to a restaurant where a middle-aged, big-boned waitress, like Emma, talks of her own husband: "He too is a little man, and sits up as small as you. When he is bad, I peek him up, I stand him on the mantelpiece." Eugene pays for his and the Spaniard's coffee with his last penny, having only a streetcar token left, and that to take him back to Emma—earthly, motherly Emma, who waits, popping grapes into her mouth. Even the wandering Spaniard, at last glance, seems to be searching the sky for the feminine moon.

Facing death, R. J. Bowman in "Death of a Traveling Salesman" craves the comfort of the hearth he discovers in a backwoods cabin. Weary and sick, he realizes how far he has wandered from home and his grandmother's feather bed. When he wrecks his car at the beginning of the story, he ironically commences his return to the maternal domain: the car comes to rest in "a tangle of immense grapevines as thick as his arm, which caught it and held it, rocked it like a grotesque child in a dark cradle." Bowman's recognition of the awful cost to the wanderer who never recovers the loving, maternal world comes at the end literally with a heartburst of pain.

Only a very few of the characters in Miss Welty's fiction, female or male, steadfastly confront themselves as individuals separated from the clan, the natural life of the flesh. Some of these live out their lives in the heroic confrontation, but others move beyond the defiant, "masculine" impulse to an active acceptance of life that demonstrates a type of heroism I find expressly feminine. Of course, wise acceptance arrived at by one who has completed the tasks of the hero is, as Jung and Joseph Campbell have shown, typically the goal of the heroic quest. The archetypal adventure leads from the connection with the mother through the trials of initiation to an understanding of oneself and one's relation to the universe. At last, knowledge replaces ignorance, and the individual consciousness is reconciled with the universal.[9] Clearly the consequence of such harmony is a life that contains both one's separateness in time and one's enduring link with what I have called the matriarchal, imperishable world of nature.

George Fairchild and Jack Renfro perhaps best exemplify the individual achievement and self-sacrifice that distinguish the male characters who go through the stages of separation and heroic test, and then return to accept the ties of the family. Marrying Robbie Reid and leaving Shellmound, George establishes his difference from the Fairchild clan. What is more, he heroically faces death when he throws himself over the young cousin Maureen, who had caught her foot on the trestle just as the Yellow Dog approached. To Robbie his action appeared reckless, a kind of golden, masculine vaunting that taunted death and frustrated her attempts to protect him. But of course, his risk is needful; it makes him a "solid man, going through the world, a husband," and, as Ellen sees, it is the enabling act of his capacity for love.

George's motion to save Maureen resembles Loch's ef-

---

9. *The Hero with a Thousand Faces* (1949; rpt. New York: Meridian-World, 1967), p. 238.

fort to revive Easter. Both lifesavers perform heroically and in doing so prove their universal worth, assuring the continuance of the life cycle—literally and symbolically. That George's risk is real is underscored by the later report of the train's hitting the mysterious girl Ellen first sees in the woods. That his heroic risk subserves the generative principle is intimated not only by the sexual image of his prone body stretched across Maureen but by the information that after the train episode, he had found and slept with the strange girl, who is thus linked with Maureen by the manner of her death. She is also linked with Ellen, who at times feels herself to be the mother of the world and imagines the girl as a wonderfully beautiful daughter. Except for George, Ellen alone sees her, standing motionless in the woods as if she were in "an ancient place," as if she were "someone who lived in the woods." To Ellen, she is startlingly beautiful, with skin "white to transparency" and a soiled cheek and leafy hair that hint of a "key to all poetry." This strange, unnamed girl suggests an immortal goddess who as nature never dies but in human form does and is reborn. She resembles the white goddess described by Robert Graves or Frazer's Diana at Nemi, both of whom are aspects of the great Mother Goddess, the personification of all reproductive energies of nature.

When Ellen dances with George at the wedding party, she feels restored by his presence—he is the rare one who understands and can relieve her heart's overflow. Heroic risk, death, restoration of Ellen in the sacred grove of Shellmound—these are the essential cycles. Youthful Dabney wonders at one point why "death could be a part of a question about the crops." Ellen and George, on the other hand, understand the necessary flow between life and death, love and separateness. At the novel's conclusion,

George gives signs that the lessons of the wedding week have not been lost on him. He talks of returning with Robbie to the Grove, the nearby plantation where Primrose and Jim Allen live, of having a garden and a cow. Robbie's mood too has tempered, and she laughs gently as the family talks of their return. But George's vision of himself outside the family and his unblinking recognition of what's in the world—the knowledge that every creature lives on the death of another—assure that he will never return to the unconscious bliss of the clan. He consents however to be a mediator between the threatening outside world (he defends against the train) and the devouring inside world of kin. George understands and accepts that the house he will come home to has rats and ghosts, but that it also contains the springs that nourish life.

In the final scene a shooting golden star, like George's dazzling deed, transfixes Laura and India for the moment of its fall. Laura especially is excited by its beauty, appropriately so since she is the one whose papa has taken her on trips, the one who knows geography beyond the confines of Shellmound. But in the radiant night that covers the picnicking family, the star has only a momentary place. In the sky the "lady moon, with a side of her hair gone, was rising."

Jack Renfro is a different kind of hero from George Fairchild; he is an optimist, and perhaps not a hero at all. He lacks George's sense of conscious separateness from the family, but he also transcends the mindless wanderer's separateness—the animal boyishness of the natural world. He seems to me to be pure of heart, though of course that is exactly what Ellen thinks of George. But George moves always in the shadow of the dead brother Denis whereas Jack, who is no unbroken left-hander like

George, acts intuitively, exuberantly as savior of the family. Like Phoenix Jackson he knows instinctively of the love and sacrifice that go beyond the natural to the human world, where he performs heroically, but with an unlearned grace. Fighting Curley Stovall, he defends the family's honor, fittingly signified by the golden wedding ring that is the family's treasure. His potency brings green growth to the fields and a new baby into the family, but it is in his loving presence—in this so unlike King McLain—that he sustains Gloria and all the others. Capable of deep feeling if not reflection, he pays dearly for his heroic moment when Judge Moody sentences him for "aggravated battery" to the penitentiary. He learns, as do the others, that the worst punishment there is is being separated from those you love. Gloria is no doubt right when she protests that Jack is believing and blind, but in losing his freedom and being separated from the security of the clan, he gets to the truth first. And the truth is that the good life is right in Banner, with his teacher Gloria and baby Lady May and the whole extended human chain of family and friends. Jack's venturing and coming back sharpen his sensibility, however, so that unlike the tribe he can *love* Miss Julia, having heard her story, and he can even lead Gloria to an accommodation with the Beechams and Renfros.

Gloria, like other Welty outsiders who have the heroic impulse toward separateness but who have not quite learned how to accept and love, looks upon the family group with a mixture of jealousy and revulsion. From the outside view families are like flocks of birds, always eating, chattering, copulating, getting born and dying, like the pigeons Laurel remembers in *The Optimist's Daughter*: "sticking beaks down each other's throats, eating out of each other's craws, swallowing down all over again what had been swallowed before." When Robbie first approaches Shellmound, she thinks: "They were probably back there eating—they always were. . . . They were all back there in oblivion eating." To little girls with a dream of love, like the child in "A Memory," the physicality of the human bond is horrifying—the family of bathers are carnal and ugly.

Some such outsiders persist in their exalted expectation of human life to the very end. These are brave, tragic outsiders, heroes like Julia Percival Mortimer, who go through life holding to private dreams and separate selves, fighting the human chains that imprison the individual. They condemn mere being in favor of doing and knowing and judge the natural matriarchal world to be innocent and ignorant, a dragon to be attacked. Both Miss Julia and, to a great extent, Becky McKelva, demand that life have purpose, and they do not waver or flag in pursuing it. They act the St. George or Perseus in their aggressive, masculine advance against monstrous Nature, which brutishly accepts or forgives, or ignores individual victory or death. An Appolonian type, Julia Mortimer "didn't want anybody left in the dark, not about anything," according to Gloria. "She wanted everything brought out in the wide open, to see and be known." Miss Julia, of course, once set herself against a cyclone, refusing to dismiss class even when the schoolhouse roof flew off. She taught on, above the storm, insisting to the children that the school was the best place to be. But the citizens of Banner at last proved a more formidable opponent than the tornado. Most took her effort to turn them into doctors, lawyers and "all else," to make them stop worshipping themselves and look outward beyond Banner, as their cross to bear until she released them from the schoolhouse. From Beulah's point of view, "Miss Julia was as wrong as you could ever hope about the best place to be!"

At her death Julia Mortimer is still undaunted and unreconciled, even after the mortification of her final days when she was tied down, denied books or pen and paper. "What was the trip for?" she demands to know. But Willy Trimble was the wrong one to ask. So in fact were Judge McKelva and Laurel the wrong ones for Becky to ask for explanations of the meaning of her dying. The threshold of death is precisely the boundary of the heroic; beyond it lies the diminishment of the individual in the human comedy. Laurel understands this lesson very well in the story of her mother's youthful attempt to get her own dying father to a hospital in Baltimore: "Baltimore was as far a place as you could go with those you loved, and it was where they left you."

Laurel McKelva Hand is, in fact, an unusual human being, one of a small group of characters who go through all the stages of humanness we have been looking at. She moves from childlike innocence through the ease of pure loving, through seeing the hideous face of the living world, to acceptance, back at last to the material, phenomenal world of nature—but with a mindful love of it. She completes the journey of individuation, a path not so well worn in life or fiction.

As a child, she is part of the world of the mothers—Becky and Grandmother Thurston, a self-contained, sufficient world of sewing rooms, gardens, family. For all her later loneliness, Becky holds Beulah Renfro's view that "up home" was the best place on earth to be. To be sure, Laurel's youthful apprehension of the carnality and coarseness of life gives an early sign of her self-consciousness, but she does not let the vision touch her. It is the pigeons, she thinks, not she and her family who are hideous. When she marries Philip Hand, she revels in a dream of perfect love, like a Rosamond loving Jamie Lockhart in the darkness or Snowdie Hudson blinded by the brilliance of King. If Phil had lived, he might have helped Laurel understand the link between the dream and the world, how to move from the periphery of life or a sketch into the essential design, that is, how to move out of the darkness. But it is not until years later when she returns to Mount Salus that she finally *sees* the world, her family, and herself within both.

Laurel, very much Becky's daughter, respects her mother's heroic effort to impose purpose on life, just as Judge Moody respected Miss Julia. But after Becky's death Laurel and her father live on, and Fay appears. Laurel knows that Fay was her mother's horror, like jaybirds and weeds, but that Fay was inevitable. Looking outward with a plenary vision, Laurel discovers that she has had two mothers—Becky, who gave a dream of mastery and order, and stepmother Fay, who was always there, as eternal as the weather.

She could have avoided claiming kin with Fay if she had stayed inside a fortress of innocence, or timidity, or proud heroism, but she wanted intensely to live. Like Virgie Rainey she suspects no fortress would ever come down, "except before hard little horns, a rush and a stampede of the pure wish to live." So the fortress opens, she lets a bird fly in, just as Robbie Reid does at Shellmound. She invites death into the house so she can get at the lusty, exuberant world's bodiness. Like her optimistic father, she accepts it all, but with a keen sensibility of life's conditions. She discovers the doubleness of experience and in doing so uncovers a design of wholeness, the realization, as Carl Jung writes, that the self is both God and animal—not merely the empirical being but the total being, which is rooted in one's animal nature and reaches out beyond the human toward the divine. It is a wholeness that "implies a tremendous tension of opposites paradoxically at one with themselves."[10]

Of course, the feeling and seeing person always harbors this secret of duality. Sometimes we see it expressed in Miss Welty's fiction in the figure of a man, like Judge McKelva, old Mr. Marblehall, or Clement Musgrove, married to two antithetical wives. But among the characters who seem finally most at peace and most knowing in the double world are Laurel, Ellen Fairchild, and Virgie Rainey. Although we are told only a little of Ellen's life before she became a Fairchild, the pattern is clear. She is an early version of daughter Shelley and perhaps even of Laura McRaven—bookish, dreamy, modest in her youth. Back in Virginia, she sang with a little choral society of unmarried ladies, "I Would That My Love." Quite early, however, Ellen's adolescent dream of love is tempered by experience. Not marriage but childbirth, which she faced without doctor or mother, with Partheny alone, initiates her into the world of the flesh, a world she never wholly belongs to or is apart from. Like Virgie Rainey looking at the picture of Perseus holding the head of the Medusa, she looks at the new bride and groom in the family, seeing in Dabney a vision first of the hopeful choral singer and then of the young girl of the bayou woods, victimized and dead. Her vision of the initiation that awaits Dabney is characteristically feminine and conforms exactly to the death

10. *Symbols of Transformation*, trans. R. F. C. Hull (1956; rpt. New York: Harper Torchbooks, 1962), II, 303.

cycle of the Great Eleusinian Mysteries of the ancient world. In this the maiden Kore, Demeter's daughter and second self, is carried away and raped by death. The prospect, in terms of the myth and of Ellen's vision seems grim, but Ellen accepts it, for she knows the rape-death will evolve ultimately into rebirth.

After Dabney's wedding, waltzing past a tree hung with a golden lantern and mistletoe—a golden bough—Ellen shines forth as an embodiment of the matriarchal principle of biological life, carrying as she does a child within her. She has reached beyond the merely human and held a dream, but, passionate woman that she is, she has lovingly sacrificed it to be Ellen Fairchild, to be part of the repeating cycles of this earth. In doing so, she expresses as well a feminine principle of mindful love that serenely enfolds heroic acts. Finally, "she loved what was pure at its heart, better than what was understood."

In his commentary on the Psyche myth as an archetype of the feminine consciousness, Neumann observes that Psyche's act of looking on the face of her lover, the act of illumination, appears to be a "masculine" deed, resembling that of the hero. But there is a crucial difference in her heroism: whereas the male hero goes on from his act of heroic slaying to conquer the world, "Psyche's subsequent development is nothing other than an attempt to transcend, through suffering and struggle, the separation accomplished by her act. On a new plane, that is, in love and full consciousness, she strives to be reunited with him who had been separated from her and make whole again by a new union what necessity had impelled her to sacrifice." Unlike the gods who love mortals, experiencing only desire and pleasure, Psyche *is* mortal, the soul of the mortal, and as Neumann says, for her, "love as an expression of feminine wholeness is not possible in the dark, as a merely unconscious process; an authentic encounter with another involves consciousness, hence also the aspect of suffering and separation."[11]

I think Neumann's study bears directly on the situation of characters like Laurel, Ellen, and, especially, Virgie Rainey, all of whom have a passionate regard for life that by necessity gives them a sense of themselves as separate human beings. Virgie's passion is obvious even in childhood—as a little girl who plucks great magnolia blossoms and eats strange sandwiches, who is filled with vitality and wildness, the natural daughter of "Katie Blazes" and, we suspect, King McLain. As the star pupil of her piano teacher Miss Eckhart, she accepted the double vision which her teacher offered, *the* Beethoven of Miss Eckhart, who had absorbed the hero and the sacrificed self. But the child Virgie had not found *her* Beethoven, her reconciliation with an earth filled with opposites. Early she had set out to see the world but had returned to Morgana, disappointed in love, frustrated at finding so little of what she had dreamed of. She takes up the routine tasks of the farm and her work, which leave her with burned, scarred hands that the complacent wives of Morgana make "stigmata of something at odds in her womanhood." There are even times when she yearns for release from her sightedness, wishing as she pulls the udders of the cow for "the blindness that lay inside the beast." But her greater dread is to live just such a life, inured to feeling—"to callous over, go opaque."

At the conclusion of *The Golden Apples*, Virgie has claimed for herself the life Miss Eckhart offered. Taking

---

11. Neumann, *Amor and Psyche*, pp. 83–85.

Medusa slain and Perseus, slayer, as one's sacrificed innocence and one's vaunting egoism, she also takes the dragon's blood, the severance of heart's need and will's desire. To live in the moment, in time, she accepts the burden of maintaining the tension of opposites. Miss Katie once said every woman should have a line drawn through her body—the long way—so as to have a side "to feel and know, and a side to stop it, to be waited on, finally." But for Virgie the side of feeling and knowing impels her into the world in search of love, a world of human, sensuous connectedness. Only there can she feel "the air's and the earth's fuming breath" or hope to possess earth's "hideous and delectable" treasures.

One might regard Virgie's turning to the material world, what I have earlier called the matriarchal world, as an intellectual and spiritual regression. I expect Julia Mortimer would so regard it. But Virgie, like Laurel and even Ellen, does not blindly become one with Mother Earth. Rather, she exemplifies what Neumann describes as the archetype of psychic development. By preferring the sensuous beauty of earth to abstract knowledge, she reunites herself with the feminine in her nature. "Her 'old' femininity enters into a new phase." [12]

Virgie's example offers a convenient conclusion to what I admit is a very tentative topography of Eduora Welty's fictional world. I must report that this world looms up, mysterious and elusive, exactly in proportion to a scheming analyst's determination to plot it on a graph. Rich with physical texture and enlivened with human beings whose secret cannot be plucked out and plotted, this world is engaging and infectious, and profoundly re-

---

12. *Ibid.*, p. 127.

vealing of life. Having persisted this far in an analysis of it, however, I should like to offer the following observations.

Quite aside from the matter of whether a given character is male or female, we find represented in Miss Welty's fiction several overlapping realms of human enterprise and personality. One is that of biological life, which I have characterized as matriarchal, involving as it does those characters (or those early stages of psychological development) in which the individual's identity is derived from his or her relation to the mother or the family. Another is the realm of the individual, the heroic and egoistic, what I have called the masculine principle, with its emphasis on the will and other-worldliness. Finally, there is the realm of the feminine, in which knowledge and transcendence are transferred back to the natural earth and are realized in its materiality.

Thus the basis of my title is revealed. Having mastered arithmetic, I figure that the presence of the *matriarchal* and *feminine* gives two for the women, and the *masculine*, one for the men—hence woman's world, man's place. But before anyone asks which shell I tucked the patriarchs under, let me draw a conclusion thus: Despite depth of feeling or stages of maturity, the characters moving through Miss Welty's stories are celebrated for themselves, created surely out of a tolerant and benevolent love of their diversity and fickleness. But the loving outside view of the author who engenders them gives form finally to the inside view, which is that the characters who get to the truth have a Weltian, feminine vision—or psyche.

On the psychological level, they see the world with androgynous eyes, or, as Neumann writes, they are guided not by the ego but by the totality. Imagistically, they typically see by the light of the moon, for, unlike the sun, the moon's continually changing aspects suggest coexistent opposites.[13] In an anthropological sense, these characters are connected with the origins of humanness and show up the lonely separateness of patriarchs and heroes. They are as well a post-existential breed who expose the limits of the individual will. More religious than philosophical, they shun the Gnostic impulse, trusting finally in the condition of this world rather than yearning for some other.

They point up a historical perspective that is more Southern than American, embodying as they do the qualities Robert Heilman once identified as the Southern temper: a sense of the concrete, the elemental, the ornamental, the representative, and the totality.[14] Typical of their particular historical perspective is a respect for a family's stories. They trust these, rather than philosophy, to preserve what is distinctive and grand about the human condition. Memory will never be impervious, thinks Laurel Hand, and indeed it is memory, not reason, that brings the achievements and lessons of the past into the present moment.

The literary mode most congenial to these Weltian characters is an amiable realism—humor, which depends for its life on the achieved world of appearance in the stories, what Miss Welty writes of as place in fiction. They belong finally to luminous, exuberant comedy, not tragedy. It has always seemed to me that Faulkner believed too deeply in Joe Christmas's condition really to

---

13. See Adrienne Rich on symbols associated with the moon in *Of Woman Born* (New York: Norton, 1976), p. 125.

14. "The Southern Temper," in *Southern Renascence*, ed. Louis D. Rubin, Jr., and Robert D. Jacobs (Baltimore: Johns Hopkins Press, 1953), p. 3.

trust equally in Lena Grove's; but in Miss Welty's fiction we find an unfaltering trust in Phoenix Jackson's journey or Jack Renfro's or Virgie Rainey's—journeys which move across battlefields and on, journeys that give us all, women and men alike, a cause for rejoicing.

Precision and Reticence:
Eudora Welty's Poetic Vision

WILLIAM JAY SMITH

ISAK DINESEN, IN INTRODUCING her-
self, used to say that she came from a long line of story-
tellers. Eudora Welty comes from a similar long line, and
her work reminds us on every page of the qualities of the
ancient art of storytelling, which are often lost sight of
today. The ancient storyteller was a poet, and to hold the
attention of his listeners he made use of those age-old
rhythmic and incantatory devices that we still find in
folktales. The action of his story might be endlessly complicated, but he had to make every bit of it immediately
clear and memorable. His tale was often lyrical, and at
moments of great tension it would break into pure song.
All the senses were brought into play so that the listener
could literally see the action as it unfolded, smell the evil
villain, and touch the soft wings of birds that lifted him
from the earth. In a moving passage to which I shall return, Eudora Welty in *The Optimist's Daughter* evokes
the storyteller's voice when she describes the protagonist
remembering the sound of her parents reading to each
other:

When Laurel was a child, in this room and in this bed where she
lay now, she closed her eyes like this and the rhythmic, nighttime

78

sound of the two beloved reading voices came rising in turn up the stairs every night to reach her. She could hardly fall asleep, she tried to keep awake, for pleasure. She cared for her own books, but she cared more for theirs, which meant their voices. In the lateness of the night, their two voices reading to each other where she could hear them, never letting a silence divide or interrupt them, combined into one unceasing voice and wrapped her around as she listened, as still as if she were asleep. She was sent to sleep under a velvety cloak of words, richly patterned and stitched with gold, straight out of a fairy tale, while they went reading on into her dreams.

As Katherine Anne Porter long ago remarked, Eudora Welty has "an ear sharp, shrewd, and true as a tuning fork." She has such control of the speech that she records that like the true poet she makes her reader read with exactly the rhythm that she chooses, a rhythm that may range all the way from the lickety-split monologue of the heroine of "Why I Live at the P.O."—

I was getting along fine with Mama, Papa-Daddy and Uncle Rondo until my sister Stella-Rondo just separated from her husband and came back home again. Mr. Whitaker! Of course I went with Mr. Whitaker first, when he first appeared here in China Grove, taking "Pose Yourself" photos, and Stella-Rondo broke us up. Told him I was one-sided. Bigger on one side than the other, which is a deliberate, calculated falsehood: I'm the same. Stella-Rondo is exactly twelve months to the day younger than I am and for that reason she's spoiled.

—to the somber, terrifying down-beat in the concluding words of the murderer in "Where Is the Voice Coming From?"—

Once, I run away from home. And there was a ad for me, come to be printed in our county weekly. My mother paid for it. It was from her. It says: "Son: you are not being hunted for anything but to find you." That time, I come on back home.

But people are dead now.

And it's so hot. Without it even being August yet.

Anyways, I seen him fall. I was evermore the one.

So I reach me down my old guitar off the nail in the wall. 'Cause I've got my guitar, what I've held onto from way back when, and I never dropped that, never lost or forgot it, never hocked it but to get it again, never give it away, and I set in my chair, with nobody home but me, and I start to play, and sing a-down. And sing a-down, down, down. Sing a-down, down, down, down. Down.

We could all make an anthology of the voices from Miss Welty's writing. Once we have heard them, they remain with us for a lifetime. But I wish to call attention not to the obvious surface aural appeal of the stories, but rather to the deeper metaphor-making genius that places Eudora Welty in the oldest tradition of the poet-storyteller.

In China in the eleventh century Wei T'ai put down the following observation: "Poetry presents the thing in order to convey the feeling. It should be precise about the thing and reticent about the feeling, for as soon as the mind responds and connects with the thing the feeling shows in the words; this is how poetry enters deeply into us." Let us examine this precision and reticence and their poetical effect in the work of Eudora Welty, first in a small piece, a poem printed twenty years ago in *The New Yorker*. Miss Welty had not intended this for publication, but had sent it in a letter to her friend Howard Moss, the poetry editor, who felt that its charm demanded a public, as well as a private, audience:

A FLOCK OF GUINEA HENS SEEN FROM A CAR

The lute and the pear are your half sisters,
The mackerel moon a full first cousin,
And you were born to appear seemly, even when running on
    guinea legs,
As maiden-formed, as single-minded as raindrops,
Ellipses, small homebodies of great orbits (little knots at the back
    like apron strings),
Perfected, sealed off, engraved like a dozen perfect consciences,
As egglike as the eggs you know best, triumphantly speckled . . .
But fast!
Side-eyed with emancipation, no more lost than a string of pearls
    are lost from one another,
You cross the road in the teeth of Pontiacs
As over a threshold, into waving, gregarious grasses,
Welcome wherever you go—the Guinea Sisters.

Bobbins with the threads of innumerable visits behind you,
As light on your feet
As the daughters of Mr. Barrett of Wimpole Street,
Do you ever wonder where Africa has fled?
Is the strangeness of your origins packed tight in those little
    nutmeg heads; so ceremonious, partly naked?
Is there time to ask each other what became of the family wings?
Do you dream?
Princess of Dapple,
Princess of Moonlight,
Princess of Conch,
Princess of Guinealand,
Though you roost in the care of S. Thomas Truly, Rt. 1
(There went his mailbox flying by),
The whole world knows you've never yet given up the secrets of
    where you've hidden your nests.[1]

This piece possesses in miniature, as in a locket almost,

---

1. *The New Yorker*, XXXIII, No. 5, p. 35.

all the qualities found in Eudora Welty's entire work—its spontaneity, its exuberance, its triumphant comic spirit, its careful characterization, its lilt, its reverence, its underlying wonder and mystery. I am reminded here of what Paul Valéry once said of Colette. While others have to work at writing, said Valéry, to Colette it comes naturally. And so it seems to come to Eudora Welty, so different from Colette and yet so close to her in spirit. From both of them the observed world flows as from a fountain; there is never the slightest hint of the pump. This little poem is a throwaway number, tossed off, seemingly thrown right out the window of the car in which it was written; and yet it tells us what a wonderful universe we inhabit where such strange, exotic, and beautiful creatures can roost right next door—in the care of yours, Thomas Truly. Certainly Eudora Welty is in this instance precise about the thing so that we have before us, done with perfect brush strokes, the picture of a flock of guinea hens running across the road, and she is just as reticent about the feeling; indeed, the thing observed is reticence itself:

The whole world knows you've never yet given up the secret of
  where you've hidden your nests.

Just as the guinea hens do not reveal the hiding place of their nests so the feeling here is held back and made all the stronger by being put wholly into the thing observed. This is a wonderful bit of fluff, of light verse, and yet it is at the same time serious, as all light verse must be. (All writing, as Miss Welty frequently reminds us, is serious if it is any good.) What a magnificent use of apostrophe and anticlimax, of metaphor and simile, and, of course, of personification, the human reference, which gives depth and dimension and resonance:

Ellipses, small homebodies of great orbits (little knots at the back
  like apron strings),
Perfected, sealed off, engraved like a dozen perfect consciences
  . . .
You cross the road in the teeth of Pontiacs
As over a threshold, into waving, gregarious grasses,
Welcome wherever you go—the Guinea Sisters.

In speaking of the guinea hens as sisters, Miss Welty—perhaps instinctively, for nothing in this verse seems at all studied—evokes an ancient tradition. The Greeks spoke of guinea fowl as "Meleagridae," because it was thought that Meleager's sisters had been transformed into guinea hens.

I am not the first to call attention to Eudora Welty's awareness of the visual and plastic arts. In connection with her miniature of guinea hens, I think of what she once wrote about the Spanish sculptor José de Creeft, whose *taille directe*, his method of working directly in stone, she admires. She commented, as she observed him at work:

He also occupied himself with a whole colony of two- and three-inch high clay figures which he brought with him. A marvelous and sympathetic sense of the absurd in man could account for the playful but astonishing and keen distortions in these figures, which are a kind of thinking in clay. A godlike affection as well as a devastating devil-glance has perpetrated these. Caricature can be the sign of the whole of tolerance—and limitless delight in the unending possibilities of form. And the absurd is often the last gate before the most unexplored fields of the imagination—where any undreamed of beauty might be. . . . All of life has its place in de Creeft's frame of vision—life as of-the-moment, as a smile, yet enduring as stone is. A truth is shown here—that the most intimate, fragile, transitory expression of life is as real and enduring as basic rock—that nothing in life can be lost—the most playful moments, equally with the most serious, endure and have their place.

All of life has its place in Eudora Welty's frame of vision also, and nowhere is this more evident than in *The Optimist's Daughter*, where the frame of vision encompasses vision itself. The thing seen is sight. In his fine essay "Speech and Silence" James Boatwright says:

Most novels of course *contain* speech and silence, but *Losing Battles* seems to me a special case, in that it is not only an overwhelming *gathering* of voices—dozens of them—shouting, whispering, intoning and preaching thousands of words, thousands of sentences, among them some of the funniest, saddest, hardest and most truthful we are likely to hear anywhere—*Losing Battles* not only *is* the voices, and the silences that sometimes lie between them, ticking like time bombs: it is also *about* speech and silence, about these profoundly curious phenomena. In its unfolding, the novel suggests to us, for the most part obliquely, dramatically, *what to make of* speech and silence.

In a similar way, *The Optimist's Daughter* is about not only all the many things both sad and funny that are seen through the eyes of the protagonist, but also about the eye itself, its function and ultimately its artistic triumph. Mr. Boatwright calls attention to the scene in *Losing Battles* when night has fallen and the family has gathered on the porch in the glare of a dangling light bulb: "For the first time, all talk was cut off, and no baby offered to cry. Silence came travelling in on solid, man-made light." In *The Optimist's Daughter* we also hear the many voices of the great human family, and perceive the same great silence, but we are aware especially of light, both natural and man-made, as the central focus of the work.

In *The Optimist's Daughter* Judge McKelva has come to New Orleans from his home in Mount Salus, Mississippi, to consult a well-known eye specialist, originally a neighbor whom he had befriended and helped through medical school, to have his eyes examined. It is early March, the time of Mardi Gras. Judge McKelva is accompanied by his silly second wife, Fay, whom he had met when she was a member of a typists' pool at a Bar convention, and his daughter, Laurel McKelva Hand, a widow in her middle forties, slightly older than Fay. Laurel, whose husband had been killed by kamikaze pilots in World War II, has come from Chicago, where she makes her living as a designer of fabrics (her most recent job has been designing a curtain for a repertory company). Judge McKelva's trouble is diagnosed immediately as a detached retina, and he is operated on at once. The two women watch over him during the succeeding days in the dark hospital room. Just as his eye is about to heal, the Judge suddenly dies, his death brought on by Fay, who in exasperation shakes him and tries to get him up. The two women accompany the body back to Mount Salus, where it is laid out in the family library to be viewed by the townspeople, and by members of Fay's family, who have driven over from Texas. Judge McKelva is buried not in the old section of the town cemetery next to his first wife, but in the new section near the interstate in a plot chosen by Fay. While Fay departs with her family for a few days, Laurel, alone in the house, struggles to come to terms with the deaths of her parents and of her husband. Just before she leaves the house, she happens in a kitchen closet on her mother's breadboard, which had been carved by her husband. She finds it marred by the gouges that Fay has made by cracking walnuts on it. She lifts the breadboard to strike Fay, who appears, but then stops, realizing that Fay is like a child, incapable of understanding anything that has happened to her. Laurel leaves for Chicago, free of the burden of the past but at the same time restored by having discovered "the whole story, the whole solid past." Memory for her then "lived not in initial possession but in the freed hands, pardoned and freed, and in the heart that can empty but fill again, in the patterns restored by dreams."

The book is divided into four parts like the four panels of an altarpiece. The first is the hospital with its concentration on the inner vision, on the eye itself; the second is the return to Mount Salus, the outer vision, the eye's view of the funeral; the third, the protagonist's dark night, the focus within the house and within the self; and finally the outer and inner meeting, with the protagonist's confrontation of her stepmother and the final resolution, the development in the protagonist of a deep inner vision and of real insight.

All the dictionary meanings of the word "eye" and their symbolic implications have full play from the very first paragraph when the nurse shows the Judge, together with his wife and daughter, into the windowless room for the optical examination, holding in his hand the glasses that he customarily wears on a ribbon. The overlying levels of verbal play are so complex and constitute such a luminous unity that they reveal themselves only after several readings. Judge McKelva's trouble begins when on his porch he looks out at the fig tree in his yard, and finds that the homemade reflectors, the rounds of tin, placed on the tree to frighten off the birds, are giving off flashes. These homemade reflectors become the outer reflection of the retina detached from the eyeball and swinging in dislocation. After the Judge's death our attention is called once again to the bird-frighteners:

> As Laurel walked with Miss Adele toward her own opening in the hedge, there could be heard a softer sound than the singing from the dogwood tree. It was rhythmic but faint, as from the shaking of a tambourine.
> "Little mischiefs! Will you look at them showing off," said Miss Adele.
> A cardinal took his dipping flight into the fig tree and brushed wings with a bird-frightener, and it crashed faintly. Another cardinal followed, then a small band of them. Those thin shimmering discs were polished, rain-bright, and the redbirds, all rival cocks, were flying at their tantalizing reflections. At the tiny crash the birds would cut a figure in the air and tilt in again, then again.
> "Oh, it's a game, isn't it, nothing but a game!" Miss Adele said, stepping gracefully into her own backyard.

But for Laurel this is more than a game; it is a grim reminder of the blood in her father's eyeball and of the Japanese kamikaze pilots who came down to kill her husband in World War II. The detached retina is again reflected in the double baskets which Laurel cups together to enclose the chimney swift that has flown down the chimney of the house, looking when it is finally caught "eyeless, unborn, so still was it holding."

The Optimist's Daughter contains some of Eudora Welty's most brilliant descriptive writing, but none of it is merely for decoration; all of it has an important part in moving the story forward. Here is the Judge's room at the hospital:

> This was like a nowhere. Even what could be seen from the high window might have been the rooftops of any city, colorless and tarpatched, with here and there small mirrors of rainwater. At

first, she did not realize she could see the bridge—it stood out there dull in the distance, its function hardly evident, as if it were only another building. The river was not visible. She lowered the blind against the wide white sky that reflected it. It seemed to her that the grayed-down, anonymous room might be some reflection itself of Judge McKelva's "disturbance," his dislocated vision that had brought him there.

Laurel rushes into the room when her father is dying:

> The door stood wide open, and inside the room's darkness a watery constellation hung, throbbing and near. She was looking straight out at the whole Mississippi River Bridge in lights. She found her way, the night light burning.

The Venetian blind has fallen, and as she gazes out, she in reality gazes into the eyeball of her father, whose life is ebbing away. As the train pulls out of New Orleans on to Lake Pontchartrain, Laurel finds her own reflection in the windowpane:

> Set deep in the swamp, where the black trees were welling with buds like red drops, was one low beech that had kept its last year's leaves, and it appeared to Laurel to travel along with their train, gliding at a magic speed through the cypresses they left behind. It was her own reflection in the windowpane—the beech tree was her head. Now it was gone. As the train left the black swamp and pulled out into the space of Pontchartrain, the window filled with a featureless sky over pale smooth water, where a seagull was hanging with wings fixed like a stopped clock on a wall.

Laurel moves down the hospital hall like Alice down the rabbit hole:

A strange milky radiance shone in a hospital corridor at night, like moonlight on some deserted street. The whitened floor, the whitened walls and ceiling, were set with narrow bands of black receding into the distance, along which the spaced-out doors, graduated from large to small, were all closed. Laurel had never noticed the design in the tiling before, like some clue she would need to follow to get to the right place. But of course the last door on the right of the corridor, the one standing partway open as usual, was still her father's.

Laurel has indeed all the Alice qualities—a love of decorum, a hatred of noise—in contrast to Fay, the evil stepmother, whose birthday is the day of Mardi Gras, who loves noise and the sounds "of hundreds, of thousands, of people *blundering*," and who chooses a graveyard plot for her husband on the edge of the interstate highway. While Alice offers us a clear display of reason in an underground nightmare world, Laurel threads a path through an everyday world of nightmare, where in the words of Goya, echoing Addison, "When reason slumbers, monsters are created." It is only at the end of the book, having developed insight and inner vision, that she can put these monsters in their proper place.

Within the central metaphor of vision, words play an important role. For Fay, who never calls anything by name and whose family she says is no longer living, words are dead things. For her writing is typewriting. But for Laurel, words, in the slow development of insight, are crucial. While in the external scenes, words whirl busily and noisily around from person to person within "the great, interrelated family of those who never know the meaning of what has happened to them," in the scenes in which the concentration is interior, words are silent; they are liter-

ally seen, not heard. Laurel reads to her father in the afternoon in the hospital:

> *Nicholas Nickleby* had seemed as endless to her as time must
> seem to him, and it had now been arranged between them, with-
> out words, that she was to sit there beside him and read—but si-
> lently, to herself. He too was completely silent while she read.
> Without being able to see her as she sat by his side, he seemed to
> know when she turned each page, as though he kept up, through
> the succession of pages, with time, checking off moment after
> moment; and she felt it would be heartless to close her book until
> she'd read him to sleep.

In the library behind the bank of greenery where Judge
McKelva is laid out, Laurel sees the two loaded bookcases
"like a pair of old, patched velvety cloaks hung up there on
the wall." When her eye locates the set of Gibbon the color
of ashes "like a sagging sash across the shelf," she realizes
that she should have read Gibbon rather than Dickens to
her father. The books in the library, shoulder to shoulder,
"had long since made their own family." In every book she
is reminded of the voices of her father and mother reading
to each other, of "the breath of life flowing between them,
and the words of the moment riding on it that held them in
delight." In her mother's desk Laurel comes on McGuf-
fey's Fifth Reader, from which her mother, when blind in
bed, would recite the compulsive rhythms of "The
Cataract of Lodore":

> "... *Rising and leaping—*
> *Sinking and creeping,*
> *Swelling and sweeping—*
> *Showering and springing,*
> *Flying and flinging,*
> *Writhing and ringing. ...*"

The words recited from memory by her mother were a kind of defense "in some trial that seemed to be going on against her life." Now seen on the page, they rush up to Laurel illuminating the memory of her mother's last blind days. When at the end of the book Laurel stands in the driveway burning her father's letters and her mother's papers, she sees on one little scrap the words "this morning?" with "the uncompromising hook of her mother's question mark." As the words are consumed in smoke, she wants to reach for them as a child might for a coin left lying in the street, wanting only to replace the words and make them over, giving her mother new words for the vanishing ones.

Laurel's final confrontation of words brings home to us the true meaning of vision, with which the novel has been concerned. In the beginning Laurel is a designer of fabrics, attentive only to external reality, avoiding involvement with other people. She had been designing a theater curtain when she left Chicago. Now with the insight that she has gained into the nature of love and memory, she can part that curtain and look at what she sees in the breadboard fashioned by her dead husband, "the whole story, the whole solid past." Her husband Philip Hand (the names of all the characters are significant) was a craftsman, and now in the fullness of memory Laurel is truly married to her craft. While early in the book she sees her head reflected in the windowpane of the train as a beech tree with last year's leaves, she departs in the end from her home town in the simple glory of her name—Laurel, green and growing—waved to by the schoolchildren, unknown to her but saluting the true artist that she has become.

Place has its place here as in all Miss Welty's work: there

are masterly descriptions of the meeting of water and sky, earth and air, and of the birds that bring them together. Birds move constantly in and out, and their symbolic importance emerges at key moments in the story. Pigeons come to Laurel's mind when she remembers her childhood vacations "up home" in West Virginia with her mother and grandmother:

Laurel had kept the pigeons under eye in their pigeon house and had already seen a pair of them sticking their beaks down each other's throats, gagging each other, eating out of each other's craws, swallowing down all over again what had been swallowed before: they were taking turns. The first time, she hoped they might never do it again, but they did it again next day while the other pigeons copied them. They convinced her that they could not escape each other and could not themselves be escaped from. So when the pigeons flew down, she tried to position herself behind her grandmother's skirt, which was long and black, but her grandmother said again, "They're just hungry, like we are."

On the train on the way down to be married in New Orleans, Laurel and Philip gaze out on the confluence of the Ohio and the Mississippi:

They were looking down from a great elevation and all they saw was at the point of coming together, the bare trees marching in from the horizon, the rivers moving into one, and as he touched her arm she looked up with him and saw the long, ragged, pencil-faint line of birds within the crystal of the zenith, flying in a V of their own, following the same course down. All they could see was sky, water, birds, light, and confluence. It was the whole morning world.
And they themselves were a part of the confluence.

And finally, driving death from the house, Laurel releases the chimney swift:

Something struck her face—not feathers; it was just a blow of wind. The bird was away. In the air it was nothing but a pair of wings—she saw no body any more, no tail, just a tilting crescent being drawn back into the sky.

Like the soul leaving the body, the bird becomes a brush stroke on the air, merging with light itself.

In my glancing metaphorical summary I have not discussed the most important element of the book, the characters. They are among the funniest, most moving, and at times most terrifying that Miss Welty has yet created, and, as is fitting in a work concerned with vision, are presented in distinct and powerful tableaux. If in painterly terms the hospital scenes of *The Optimist's Daughter* evoke the handling of light by Georges Latour or Vermeer, the funeral scenes call up in their combined humor and horror both Breughel and Hieronymous Bosch.

What I have been attempting to say Miss Welty has summarized herself in her foreword to *One Time, One Place*, the album of her photographs published not long after *The Optimist's Daughter* first appeared in *The New Yorker*:

We come to terms as well as we can with our lifelong exposure to the world, and we use whatever devices we may need to survive. But eventually, of course, our knowledge depends upon the living relationship between what we see going on and ourselves. If exposure is essential, still more so is the reflection. Insight doesn't happen often on the click of the moment, like a lucky snapshot, but comes in its own time and more slowly and from nowhere but within. The sharpest recognition is surely that which is charged with sympathy as well as with shock—it is a form of human vision. And that is of course a gift. We struggle through any pain or darkness in nothing but the hope that we may receive it, and through any term of work in the prayer to keep it.

In Eudora Welty's story "A Memory" a young girl who has been studying painting lies beside a lake making frames with her hands. The human scene that she discovers is not the one that she had hoped for or expected, but she is able in memory to put it down thoughtfully and clearly. The protagonist of *The Optimist's Daughter* appears to be that young girl now grown to maturity, and in the end her frame of vision can take in not only things but the infinitely extended shadows of things; she can concern herself profoundly with vision itself. *The Optimist's Daughter* may well be the most personal of Eudora Welty's works, but she has kept her eye precisely on her subject, and there is not the slightest hint of self-pity or self-glorification. And yet by being reticent about her feeling, she allows the reader's mind to respond fully to the subject. The novel is a narrative and lyrical masterpiece in which every detail is exact and significant. "Attention to detail," Osip Mandelstam said, "is the virtue of the lyric poet. Carelessness and sloppiness are the devices of lyrical sloth." Eudora Welty like the ancient lyric poet-storyteller has woven a multi-layered fabric of words, words concerned with the simplest but most important words that we know—life, death, love, and memory—and in so doing has enriched our language and given us in *The Optimist's Daughter* one of the true glories of modern literature.

Water, Wanderers, and Weddings: Love in Eudora Welty

NOEL POLK

THROUGHOUT OUR CORRESPONDENCE concerning this program, Professor Dollarhide has emphasized that it was to be a Eudora Welty "celebration." I can think of nothing finer than to celebrate her, in simple return, because her work is such a splendid celebration of us—of all the things that make our own lives joyful and sad, mysterious and profound. I am honored to be a part of these festivities, and grateful for the chance to help "celebrate" a large and complex body of fiction which is so clearly the work of an American—not just a Southern—literary genius.

I would like to address myself to a number of things which in fact have not gone unnoticed in the burgeoning body of Welty criticism—things which I designate under the general rubrics Water, Wanderers, and Weddings. Separately, they have been dealt with on a number of occasions;[1] but to my knowledge they have not yet been sufficiently treated in their relationships to one another.

---

1. Still the best full-length published study of Eudora Welty's work is Ruth M. Vande Kieft's *Eudora Welty* (New York: Twayne, 1963). Professor Vande Kieft explores many of the themes and ideas I am to discuss in this paper.

95

They are in fact frequently juxtaposed in Miss Welty's fiction, and I believe that their individual complexities can be best understood by viewing them in their interlocking triangular relationships.

Surely this audience, however, does not need to be reminded that Miss Welty's books are filled with wanderers and strangers, from R. J. Bowman, in her first published story, to Uncle Nathan in *Losing Battles*, and so I shall forego any further comment about this until later, in order to elaborate a bit more fully here at the outset what I am to mean by "water" and "weddings."

"Water" in Miss Welty's work now means to me both more and less than I had originally thought when I planned—and titled—this paper, and more and less than I can hope to account for this afternoon. I do not want to cheapen or oversimplify Miss Welty's use of water by calling it the water of life, but it does bear all of the archetypal meanings we have come to associate with it; and of course it has many obvious connections with the journey motif in her work.[2] It is the matrix, our nourishment and our source of life;[3] but it is also mysterious and fraught with peril. If it can give life, it can also take life; and so there are usually snakes and other assorted critters in Miss Welty's waters: the risk we take in living. It is frequently associated with marriage: let me point briefly to two pas-

---

2. See Carol Porter Smith's "The Journey Motif in the Collected Works of Eudora Welty" (Ph.D. diss., University of Maryland, 1971) for an interesting discussion of this theme as it appears throughout Miss Welty's work.

3. Interestingly, an early typescript of "Going to Naples," the final story in *The Bride of the Innisfallen*—a great deal of which takes place in or under or near water—bears the deleted title "The Mother of Us All." Typescript in the Mississippi Department of Archives and History.

sages in *Delta Wedding* in which Miss Welty draws our attention to the relationship between the mysterious river that runs through the plantation and Dabney's impending marriage. In the first, the bride-to-be, wandering on horseback around her father's plantation, contemplating the momentous step she is about to take, rides by the part of the river where there is a huge whirlpool; her reactions to the whirlpool and the river seem clearly to reflect her own profound agitation here on the verge of her marriage, here on the edge of the leap into life's troubled and mysterious waters:

. . . something made her get off her horse and creep to the bank and look in—she almost never did, it was so creepy and scary. This was a last chance to look before her wedding. She parted the thonged vines of the wild grapes, thick as legs, and looked in. There it was. She gazed feasting her fear on the dark, vaguely stirring water.
   There were more eyes than hers here—frog eyes—snake eyes? She listened to the silence and then heard it stir, churn, churning in the early morning. She saw how the snakes were turning and moving in the water, passing across each other just below the surface, and now and then a head horridly sticking up. The vines and the cypress roots twisted and grew together on the shore and in the water more thickly than any roots should grow, gray and red, and some roots too moved and floated like hair. On the other side, a turtle on a root opened its mouth and put its tongue out. And the whirlpool itself—could you doubt it? doubt all the stories since childhood of people white and black who had been drowned there, people that were dared to swim in this place, and of boats that would venture to the center of the pool and begin to go around and everybody fall out and go to the bottom, the boat to disappear? A beginning of vertigo seized her, until she felt herself leaning, leaning toward the whirlpool.

The second, which occurs later in the novel, after Dabney and Troy are married, is even more explicit:

Only she had not known how she could reach the love she felt already in her knowledge. In catching sight of love she had seen both banks of a river and the river rushing between—she saw everything but the way down. Even now, lying in Troy's bared arm like a drowned girl, she was timid of the element itself.

By "weddings," therefore, I mean not just the panoplied ceremony itself, which after all is only the point of departure, but the entire spectrum of things having to do with love relationships, whether they be sexual, parental, fraternal—or even, remembering last night's performance of *The Ponder Heart*, avuncular—and the acting out of those relationships in the complex domesticity of our everyday lives.

My topic, then, is love in Miss Welty's work. It seems to me a central presence there, the source at once of the joy as well as of the sorrow, of the clarity as well as of the confusion, of the despair as well as of the hope, that put Miss Welty's characters into motion—the search for or the retreat from love in any of its many forms, which manage to make of us all wanderers on this earth, and all too frequently aliens in our own homes. Her treatment of love is at the heart of much of my own response to her fiction, and it is, I believe, one of the things which helps account for her uniqueness in American letters. Many writers, of course, have examined the "Problem" of love in the twentieth century, but few have looked so intensely as Miss Welty at the kinds of things love does to us and for us in the everyday, day-to-day business of living our lives. Thus there is no sentimental clap-trap in her fiction about it, because she knows that love is hard: that it is one of the most difficult things we have to do, perhaps the most difficult thing there is, unless being loved is harder.

As an example of what I mean I might point again to *Delta Wedding*, which is not at all a portrait of a "Cloud-Cuckoo-land," as some have thought it; nor is it a simple comedy of rural manners. It is rather a subtle and toughminded rendering of all the tender savagery of family relationships: of the ferocious possessiveness of love. For underlying all the sweetness and light in that novel, underlying all the wedding preparations, the family visits back and forth, the night lights and the quilts, underlying all that togetherness and all those protestations of love is a rather grim substructure of violence and imprisonment. The head of the family, you will recall, is named Battle, and the interloper, the outsider come to take away their Helen, is named Troy. There are other examples: a Drowning Lake on the place, and a field called The Deadening. We are told that "Yazoo," the name of the river that runs by the Fairchild plantation, means "River of Death"; brother Roy, knowing that Laura can't swim, nevertheless throws her into that very river. Orrin bats a helpless bird against the wall with his father's hat, and Maureen pulls wings off of insects. Troy is threatened by a field hand with a knife; and a young girl, not connected with the family, is run over and killed by the train, the same train that had nearly run over George and Maureen. Finally, even though they are largely teasing, violence is implicit in much of their conversation. Dabney, sending Shelley to fetch Troy: "Tell him we're all mad and we'll break his neck if he's not here in a minute"; and Battle, yelling out the window to Laura and Maureen: "will you obey me and come to the table before I skin you alive and shake your bones up together and throw the sack in the bayou?" These are two of many examples. Individually, they don't mean much, of course, as we learned last night from Edna Earle; cumulatively, however, they have considerable weight. They speak of "killing and whipping," Miss Welty tells us, "in the exasperation and helplessness of much love."

And there are complementary images of prisons and cages—little ones and big ones—of prisoners escaped from Parchman and being hunted down by the dogs, of birds trapped in houses. Remember how Laura, watching the Fairchilds in action around the dinner table, is reminded of a "cage full of tropical birds her father had shown her in a zoo in a city—the sparkle of motion was like a rainbow, while it was the very thing that broke your heart, for the birds that flew were caged all the time and could not fly out." The Fairchilds move like that, she thinks, "quick and on the instant," and she wonders whether *they* are free. Dabney feels constrained by what she thinks of as the family's "solid wall of too much love," a wall that surrounds them all, keeping some people in, some out; and she interprets her family's forgiveness of her—of her breaking the night light, and especially of her daring to marry a declassé outsider—as sheer indulgence, which is in itself a way of keeping that wall, of too much love, erect, of keeping her in the family, all the while she is trying to break free.

As I've said, there's not a trace of sentimentality in *Delta Wedding*. For all of their qualities of grace and good humor, the Fairchilds are insular and proud and self-sufficient and defensive, dead set on protecting themselves from invasion from the outside. And if this is true of the affluent Fairchilds, it is even truer of the dirt-poor and ignorant Renfros of *Losing Battles*. For example, remember how ecstatic they become when they discover the possibility that Gloria, the outsider, may in fact be

Jack's first cousin, one of the family and therefore not an outsider after all, even though their marriage may be legally incestuous. Also recall the cruelty of the scene in which they gang up on her, smearing watermelon in her face to make her admit she is one of them, so that they can close the circle once again.

But the glue of love is always there; for all their individual shortcomings, the families in these two novels are strong and solid units.[4] And Miss Welty's treatment of the complexities of their daily affairs, both as a family and as individuals, suggests that we might say of hers what she said of Jane Austen's families, that they were for Jane Austen the "unit of everything worth knowing in life." Even if she doesn't herself endorse that idea completely, *Delta Wedding* and *Losing Battles* nevertheless eloquently proclaim that families are for Miss Welty, at the very least, extremely important stages upon which the large and small dramas of our lives are played out, intensified. And certainly in a general way what Miss Welty said about Jane Austen's families *is* true of hers:

Jane Austen needed only the familiar. Given: one household in the country; add its valuable neighbor—and there, under her hand, is the full presence of the world. Life, as if coming in response to a call for good sense, is instantaneously in the room, astir and in strong vocal power. Communication is convenient and constant; the day, the week, the season, fill to the brim with news and arrivals, tumult and crises, and the succeeding invitations. Everybody doing everything together—what mastery she has over the scene, the family scene! The dinner parties, the walking parties, the dances, picnics, concerts, excursions to

4. See Miss Welty's comments on this in Charles T. Bunting's "'The Interior World': An Interview with Eudora Welty," *Southern Review,* 8 (October 1972), 720.

Lyme Regis and sojourns at Bath, all give their testimony to Jane
Austen's ardent belief that the unit of everything worth knowing
in life is in the family, that family relationships are the natural
basis of every other relationship and the source of understanding
all the others.[5]

Modern literature is filled with strangers and wanderers, with outsiders who move through wastelands be-
moaning the fact that they are on the outside, and who live
out their frustrated and tragic lives beating on the doors,
trying to get inside, trying to connect.[6] We are primarily
concerned, in these works, with the outsider himself; we
see things from his point of view, and what we see is a
world in which communication among people is virtually
impossible, and in which love, if it exists at all, exists only
as a longed-for, sought-after, but unattainable ideal of
human happiness, or at the most as a fleeting, ephemeral
experience which the forces of modern civilization have
doomed from the start.

One of the many wonderful things about Miss Welty's
work is that it says to us, simply, "Shoot! Of course love is
possible." And it goes profoundly further to suggest that
the very fact that we can and do love is itself responsible
for most of our everyday problems—that the problems
caused by the ability to love are no less complicated than
those caused by the inability, simply because in our bids to
love and be loved we too often fail to give love the rest it
must have in order to keep regenerating itself. "The Key,"
for example, is a story in which a deaf-mute couple, Albert

---

5. "A Note on Jane Austen," *Shenandoah*, 20 (Spring 1969), 4.
6. Reynolds Price discusses this in connection with Miss Welty's work
in "The Onlooker, Smiling: An Early Reading of *The Optimist's Daughter*," *Shenandoah*, 20 (Spring 1969), 60.

and Ellie Morgan, have set out on a journey to find their
lost love for one another. They miss the train that is to
carry them to the restorative waters of life at Niagara
Falls. They've missed the train (or boat, if you will) long
before now, however, because they think that their love is
to be found outside themselves, at some distant place.
Their problems are primarily caused by Ellie, who is
hyper-anxious about everything, who hovers over Albert
with continual and unrelenting assurances of her love.
She wants more than anything to talk, to tell him of her
love, and she regards all silences, all privacies, all secrets,
as "unhappiness lying between them, as more than emptiness. She must worry about it, talk about it," and we
learn from the narrator that she will "sit and brood" over
their having missed the train

as over their conversations together, about every misun-
derstanding, every discussion, sometimes even about some
agreement between them that had been all settled—even about
the secret and proper separation that lies between a man and a
woman, the thing that makes them what they are in themselves,
their secret life, their memory of the past, their childhood, their
dreams. This to Ellie was unhappiness.

*The secret and proper separation that lies between a
man and a woman*—this seems to me the operative
phrase in that story, and it suggests at least one meaning of
the key itself, the one dropped so symbolically by the self-
assured stranger, which Albert picks up and holds to his
breast: it is the key, if you will, to happiness, the recognition that separateness does, must, exist, and the
acceptance of the fact that it can never be completely
overcome. I'm speaking, then, about the love that often
sours and turns to desperation, which relentlessly pursues

its beloved, trying to penetrate into the remotest and most secret corners of the other's most private heart, hoping therefore to escape its own loneliness in an actual union of the two human beings into one, which is of course impossible.

Miss Welty's work is amply peopled with outsiders— with rootless wanderers, with hitchhikers, with the lonely and the inarticulate and the frustrated, with the unloved and the unlovely. But her vision is in no way limited to their point of view; it is much more balanced. If in her work there are outsiders looking in, there are also insiders looking out:[7] Tom Harris, the traveling salesman of "The Hitch-Hikers," looking a bit wistfully at the little nameless town in which the events of that story take place, sees it as "none of . . . his, not his to keep, but belonging to the people of these towns he passed through, coming out of their rooted pasts and their mock rambles, coming out of their time. He himself had no time. He was free; helpless," while the people who feel stuck in that same town look on him as something special, even exotic, colorful in comparison with their drab lives, precisely because he seems to be so at home in the outside world: "It's marvelous," says one character of him, "the way he always gets in with somebody and then something happens."

I now would like to look a bit more closely at two short stories which were collected in *The Bride of the Innisfallen*. "No Place for You, My Love" and "The Bride of the Innisfallen" are two of Miss Welty's most complex and difficult stories, elliptical and enigmatic, whose "meaning"

---

7. See, for example, Price's *Shenandoah* article, p. 61.

has generally eluded commentators.[8] I believe, however, that an examination of them in terms of the general theme I've been outlining here can illuminate them considerably. I do not, of course, claim that this is the only way to approach these stories, or even necessarily that it is the best way; serious study of Miss Welty is too much in its infancy to allow a claim like that. I do suggest that this can be a fruitful approach, however, which can help open up at least one level of meaning of these two magnificent short stories.

In "No Place for You, My Love," two people, strangers to each other and strangers to the place, meet on a sweltering Sunday afternoon in New Orleans. They drive together in his rented convertible into the area south of New Orleans, taking a route running parallel to the Mississippi River until they reach the absolute end of the road. We are told very little about them directly. We know that he is married, that his being so makes him slip "into a groove" as he looks at her and believes that she is having an affair with a married man, and that he feels "more conventional" for having done so. Later in the story, when she asks about his wife, he replies by holding up his "iron, wooden, manicured" right hand, which we take to be a description of his wife, and, apparently, of their life together; she shifts her eyes from his hand to his face and he looks back at her "like that hand." We know also that the only reason he is in New Orleans on this particular Sunday afternoon is that his

---

8. I except, of course, Miss Welty's own comments on the first story, though they are generally of different, more technical, matters, in "How I Write," *Virginia Quarterly Review*, 31 (Winter 1955), 240–251. Alun R. Jones has some interesting things to say about both stories in his "A Frail Travelling Coincidence: Three Later Stories of Eudora Welty," in *Shenandoah*, 20 (Spring 1969), 41–53.

wife, back in Syracuse, is entertaining some college friends and does not want him "underfoot." These hints lead us to suspect that there is very little or no passion in his marriage, and that she is mostly indifferent to him, although he would have it otherwise.

We know both less and more about her, his companion on this day's wandering. The only clue we have about her past is a bruise on her temple, which she fears he can't help seeing when they dance. For all we know and he knows, she could have merely bumped her head somehow. But she feels that it sticks out "like an evil star," and her resentful hope that his seeing it will "pay him back . . . for the hand he had stuck in her face when she'd tried once to be sympathetic" implies her considerable agitation over the *real* cause of that bruise, and surely invites us to think that she has been struck by a man, perhaps her husband, perhaps even the married man her New Orleans companion suspects her of having an affair with. But the clearest indication of what is wrong back home in Ohio is the fact that she is in New Orleans indulging herself in "deliberate imperviousness." She has come to New Orleans, we thus gather, to lick some wound, to survive some experience, perhaps even rejected love, which has hurt her deeply. This may be why she so resents her companion's rejection of her proffered sympathy: opening herself up again, however tentatively, exposing her own vulnerability. "It must stick out all over me," she thinks, very self-consciously, at their first meeting in Galatoire's, though what "It" is is left to the reader's imagination:

so people think they can love me or hate me just by looking at me. How did it leave us—the old, safe, slow way people used to know of learning how one another feels, and the privilege that went

with it of shying away if it seemed best? People in love like me, I
suppose, give away the short cuts to everybody's secrets.

"Deliver us all from the naked in heart," she thinks, later
in the story.

On their drive southward they encounter hordes of
crayfish and shrimp and terrapins and turtles and al-
ligators, "crawling hides you could not penetrate with
bullets," hides she sees as "respectable and merciful."
Both covet those thick hides, though the thousands of
mosquitoes they do battle with during their ride remind us
continually that they are not armor-plated, but are in fact
two very vulnerable and hurtable human beings. So she
has retreated into a thickened hide of "deliberate imperviousness," her only protection.

These two, then, are in New Orleans to escape from, to
retreat from, unnamed and perhaps even unnameable
pressures back home. This journey is something special,
something different, something out of the ordinary for
both of them. That is why it is "Time out" in New Orleans;
and that is why they journey into such a queer place, down
to where the road ends. They are here for a respite from the
usual, the known, and for the afternoon they manage to
escape not Time and Place, but their own times, their own
places—to which they know they must eventually return.
But for now they court each other's imperviousness. They
are "immune from the world, for the time being," and at
the end of the road they come meaningfully together to
dance:

Surely even those immune from the world, for the time being,
need the touch of one another, or all is lost. Their arms encircling
each other, their bodies circling the odorous, just-nailed-down

floor, they were, at last, imperviousness in motion. They had found it, and had almost missed it: they had had to dance. They were what their separate hearts desired that day, for themselves and each other.

They spend the entire day together without ever really talking, never, so far as we are told, even exchanging names, actively resisting any impulse to get to know each other. At Baba's, at the extremity of their remove from their real lives, they dance as though "wearing masks." Returning to New Orleans he stops the car and kisses her, but it is as though he feels obliged to; it is a meaningless, perfunctory gesture; he doesn't even know whether he kisses her "gently or harshly."

The area south of New Orleans is for him a wasteland of "insignificant towns," and seems to him "like steppes, like moors, like deserts." But there is plenty of life there, happy and buoyant life, among the local people, who are laughing and boisterous everywhere; the "naked in heart," from whom she has prayed deliverance, abound: a naked baby, couples on porches—even a priest—in underwear; laughing, open faces, defenseless. Significantly, however, there is water "under everything," even under the tombs in the cemetery through which they drive. When they reach the end of the road he remarks, "If we do go any further, it'll have to be by water." But they do not go further than "land's end," do not commit themselves to the water; they do not want to grapple with its mysteries and difficulties here, out of Place, out of Time. She in fact begins to grow thirsty; her lips dry, and at Baba's she asks for a glass of water, which Baba fails to bring to her. When they return to New Orleans, at the end of their day, her only comment is, "I never got my water," which suggests that the trip has failed to nourish her in any way.

The story ends on a note even stranger than the rest of it. As he drives through New Orleans to return his rented car, he hears party-time cranking up in the bars along the street and is reminded, almost as an epiphany, of his youth as a "young and brash" student in New York, when the "shriek and horror and unholy smother of the subway had its original meaing for him as the lilt and expectation of love." This seems clearly his own comparison of the past and its exciting, limitless possibilities for love and fulfillment with his present, which finds those high expectations so hopelessly and permanently frustrated.

An early typescript of this story is entitled "The Gorgon's Head,"[9] a title which seems to have been intended to suggest that these two people have been turned to emotional stone by something, some quality of experience, that they have been forced to look at, while trying to deal with it, in their own homes. The present title, which seems to me much more evocative of the experience conveyed in the story, might be their mutual cry, an apostrophe to love, at the end of their long afternoon. Perhaps too it is the cry of that "*Something* that must have been with them all along [which] suddenly, then [at the end of their trip], was not. In a moment, tall as panic, it rose, cried like a human, and dropped back" [italics supplied].[10] Perhaps what that "something" cries is the title of the story; if so, it is a cry of despair, of panic even. For these two there is no place, not at home, not wandering free in a strange world at the bottom of the continent, for thc quality of "my love" to thrive.

---

9. Typescript in the Mississippi Department of Archives and History, Jackson.

10. See also Miss Welty's own comments on that "something" in "How I Write."

"No Place for You, My Love," then, is a serious, highly complex, and difficult short story. "The Bride of the Innisfallen," which treats a similar theme, is no less serious or complex or difficult; but it is also a piece of comic magic. The central character of "The Bride" is an American girl who if not a newlywed is apparently a recently-wed. She is fleeing from her husband, we are told, leaving London without his knowledge, on the boat-train to the coastal town of Fishguard, there to take the boat to Cork. The London that she is leaving is a dark, rainy city during a "spring that refused to flower"; it is a "black" 4 p.m. We know little about her beyond the fact that like the woman in "No Place for You, My Love" she is very self-conscious, waiting alone in the train's compartment, an early arrival, and feels that her "predicament" is obvious to anybody who looks at her. We are not told until the end of the story anything specific about what that "predicament" is, but the people who join her in the compartment—a middle-aged lady in a raincoat; a man from Connemara who shouts "*Oh* my God" at just about everything; a one-eyed Welshman who misses his station three times in the Welsh night; two Irish sweethearts; a young pregnant wife; a school girl; and a perfectly sullen little boy named Victor, who chews on the leather strap hanging at the door—their brilliant and hilarious conversation and a simply wonderful series of incidents give us clues.

The story opens as the lady in the raincoat with "salmony-pink and yellow stripes" gets on the train (the American girl is already in the compartment). She climbs aboard like a "sheltered girl," and indeed gets a "boost up from behind [which] she pretended not to need or notice" from a man we assume to be her husband; he is smaller than she is, wears a wet black suit, and has a "doll's smile" on his face: she has a "stronghold of a face." Though she is clearly the more competent of the two, she sits, the perfect wife, patiently enduring, obviously for the umpteenth time, his minutely detailed travelling instructions:

"You don't need to get out of the carriage till you get to Fishguard," the round man told her, murmuring it softly, as if he'd told her before and would tell her again. "Straight through to Fishguard, then you book a berth. You're in Cork in the morning."

She smiles sweetly, listening to him just as though he had good sense: "She looked fondly as though she had never heard of Cork, wouldn't believe it, and opened and shut her great white heavy eyelids."

She endures this, as the other passengers enter and take their seats and perforce listen to him, until the last possible moment; even after he gets off the train they clasp hands through the window until the train actually starts to move. When the man finally turns and starts to walk away, she repudiates him completely by sticking her tongue out at him and "at everything just left behind." This action relieves the tension that has been building, and establishes the comic tone of the first part of the story. As soon as she can the lady opens a pack of cigarettes, picks out one that is partly burned down already—apparently one she has almost been caught smoking—and between puffs she holds it "below her knees and turned inward to her palm," as though from long habit of hiding her smoking from her husband.

This man and woman clearly have problems, though he almost certainly doesn't know it—which is itself almost as certainly part of their problem; and the comic tone which their tender farewell helps launch does not undermine the seriousness of the problem Miss Welty is treating. As they stand there, in their endless farewell, they both "shine in the face like lighthouses smiling"—an image which suggests that both of those faces, the individuals behind them, keep looking out, searching, seeking to illuminate what they are looking at, while they themselves remain behind the light, in the dark, essentially unseen and unseeable: mysterious and unknowable.

Everything that happens on this trip, then, centers around things that come between husbands and wives. The incidents are many and come at us in wild and furious counterpoint; but I can mention only a few to illustrate. Immediately we learn that Victor, chewing on the leather strap, is returning to Ireland after having attended his brother's wedding, in London, that was so "grand" it has driven his poor mother to bed; and, given the number of marital problems in the story, that ceremony, the trouble and expense of it, must stand as a splendid ironical contrast.

The one-eyed Welshman, continuing the conversation, asks Victor whether, in his school, he studied French; Victor replies, "Ah, them languages is no good." This in turn sets off an exchange between the Welshman and the man from Connemara over the relative merits of the Irish and English languages; the man from Connemara makes the exchange thematically important: "*Oh* my God," he says.

I have an English wife. How would she like that, I wouldn't like to know? If all at once I begun on her in Irish! How would you like it if your husband would only speak to you in Irish? Or Welsh, my God?

His question of course is, finally, about the capacity of husbands and wives to communicate with each other, and as he asks it he looks around at the young Irish sweetheart, sitting sweetly under the arched arm of her young man: she does not seem "to grasp the question" because at this stage of her love she doesn't believe that anything can go wrong, that anything can come between herself and her sweetheart.

There is a conversation between the Welshman and the man from Connemara regarding the man from Connemara's former hobby of raising birds, and particularly regarding one special talking bird, which died, he says, "Owing to conditions in England"; that condition, it is later suggested, is that English wife, who has apparently poisoned the bird, obviously in a rage because he has spent more time talking to it than to her.

Finally there are the ghosts, Lord and Lady Beagle, who haunt a Connemara castle, and who seem to represent some quintessence of the marriage bond, at least as the man from Connemara tells about them, in the cycles of their relationship:

First she comes, then he comes. . . . She comes first because she's mad, and he slow—got the dagger stuck in him, you see? Destroyed by her. She walks along, carries herself grand, not shy. Then he comes, unwilling, not touching with his feet—pulled through the air. By the dagger, you might say, like a hooked fish. Because they're a pair, himself and herself, sure as they was joined together—and while you look go leaping in the bright air, moonlight as may be, and sailing off together cozy as a couple of kites *to start it again* [italics supplied].

The sweethearts, the innocents, again cannot understand, and they are simply amazed.

On board the *Innisfallen* itself, the boat from Fishguard to Cork, after having travelled in close quarters on the train, the travellers disperse, separate themselves, and quiet prevails as each takes care of his own needs; the larger compartment for the third-class passengers is a "vortex of quiet, like a room where all brains are at work and great decisions are on the brink." There are old men, "lost as Jesus's lambs," perhaps waiting for the bar to open. The young pregnant wife, who has already told everybody how anxious she is, how much she hates traveling over water, is "as desperate as she'd feared." She "saw nothing, forgot everything, and even abandoned Victor, as if there could never be any time or place in the world but this of her suffering." The man from Connemara sprawls out asleep, though at one point he looks up to see the American girl "pinned to her chair across the room, as if he saw somebody desperate who had left her husband once, endangered herself among strangers, been turned back, and was here for the second go-round. . . ." He may be right. She simply stares back at him, motionless, lost in her own thoughts.

The next morning finds them near journey's end, on their way upriver to Cork City. In contrast to the rain and gloom of the London they left, and to the dark and foggy night of Wales they travelled through, in Ireland it is bright, "a world of sky coursing above, streaming light." And if in London spring "refused to flower," in Cork City it has flowered brilliantly:

Boughs that rocked on the hill were tipped and weighted as if with birds, which were really their own bursting and almost-bursting leaves. In all Cork today every willow stood with gold-red hair springing and falling about it, like Venus alive. Rhododendrons swam in light, leaves and flowers alike; only a shadow could separate them into colors.

This is the end of the journey; it is a new beginning, the

edge of experience, the jumping-off point—a new time, a new place, bright with expectation, blossoming with possibility. As the boat pulls into the dock someone shouts "There's a bride on board," though the shouter apparently doesn't know that there is more than one "bride"; this one, though, seems to symbolize all the bright promise of that glorious Cork morning, and clearly stands in subtle contrast to all the old married folk we have encountered in the story. Miss Welty's description of the bride is gently satiric: she stands

by the rail in a white spring hat and, over her hands, a little old-fashioned white bunny muff. She stood there all ready to be met, now come out in her own sweet time. Delight gathered all around, singing began on board, bells could by now be heard ringing urgently in the town.

Significantly, though, she is alone in her anticipation, waiting to be met. We do not see *her* off the boat, and are not told whether she is met or not. But we do see what happens to the others: the woman in the raincoat, in a beautifully understated scene, is met by a "flock of beautiful childen" and a man bigger than herself, whom she is extremely glad to see. Miss Welty refuses to explain which, if either, of the two men, the one here or the one who put her on the train in London—is actually her husband, and we can easily conclude, if we want to—and I certainly do—that the woman in the raincoat is somehow leading two lives between London and Cork, like an old Mr. Marblehall, perhaps, or, in view of the children in Cork, more like a Remarkable Mrs. Pennypacker. Doubtless she will soon be as ready to leave Cork as she was to leave London, and will again stick out her tongue in repudiation, this time of Cork. The man from Connemara disappears mysteriously into the streets with his cap set on his head at a "fairly desperate angle." And, rather sadly, the young pregnant wife is met by "old women in cloaks" and three young men who are apparently her brothers: which helps to explain why she has been so quietly desperate during the trip; there is no indication that one of the three young men could be her husband.

The American girl, on whom the final paragraphs of the story focus, is of course met by no one, and she spends the glorious spring day wandering the streets of Cork, completely free and exhilarated. But at the end of the day her real life, her "predicament," catches up with her; it begins to rain. She thinks of her husband and starts to wire him. "England was a mistake," she writes, then scratches it out, taking back "the blame but without the words." We surmise that she and her husband had gone to London, possibly from America, and apparently at her instigation, like Albert and Ellie Morgan hoping that different surroundings might nurture, reaffirm, their love for one another, and make their lives together smoother; but it obviously has not done so. The problem, apparently, is not a loss of love between them, but rather "Love with the joy being drawn out of it"—"that was loneliness," she thinks, there in London with her husband and all their complications—not "this," here in Cork, where she knows nobody. We do not know clearly what her trouble is, but it seems to be an inability to communicate to her husband some excess of joy, which she therefore has to stifle to keep from getting out of hand. She cannot tell him her "secret": perhaps, like Ellie Morgan, she tries too hard, cannot let it rest; perhaps she speaks to him in her own equivalent of Irish, a language he cannot understand. Perhaps he is indifferent to her. Perhaps, as we heard Edna Earle suggest last night, she has hugged him too hard. Her trouble, he has told her, is that she "hope[s] for too much"—from him, perhaps, from herself, from their marriage, from life. And so she has found London, too, stifling. "*I* was nearly destroyed," she thinks.

Her trip to Cork, another place, but this time without her husband, has released her from her building pressures at home, as respites from the ordinary do for us all; she is exhilarated, and wants to wire home "Don't expect me back yet." As the story ends she enters a pub, a "lovely room full of strangers"—a room full of people who don't know her and whom she doesn't know, and who therefore cannot either expect things of her or put limitations on her. It is an ending very much like that of "No Place for You, My Love," in which the man, after his wandering, remembers his youth in New York and the crowds and the shrieking clash of the subway as the "lilt and expectation of love": the bright promise, for both of them, of openness, of possibility, of freedom, of love without complication.

I would like to conclude with a quick look at *The Optimist's Daughter*, that wise short novel which is for me the most moving of all of Miss Welty's treatments of family relationships. You remember the story: because of her father's death, Laurel McKelva Hand returns from Chicago, where she has lived, for twenty years a widow, to the little Mississippi town of Mount Salus, where she grew up. During her few days in her old home, circumstances force her to recall scenes from her past, unpleasant scenes which she has long since blotted from her mind, involving the relationship between her father and mother, especially as that relationship became intensified during the years of illness preceding her mother's death. We as readers have already wondered, along with Laurel and all the Judge's friends, how on earth he could have married the cheap and vulgar Fay, the polar opposite of what we have come to believe Laurel's mother, Becky, to have been; Laurel's memory, finally freed after all those years, helps us understand. I believe that he married Fay precisely because she is so completely Becky's opposite, precisely because she makes no demands on him which he cannot fulfill. She is so easily made happy, so easily satisfied; she can be easily loved because she is so selfish and materialistic: she makes no spiritual demands upon him.

Becky, on the other hand, made plenty of demands on his spiritual resources, and without apology, though perhaps those demands were in some ways too harsh, especially in her final days. But she remains for me the touchstone of strength in the book. Laurel remembers, for example, her telling how at the age of 15 she had placed her own dying father on a raft, on a freezing, icy river—that river of life again—to take him to Baltimore for medical treatment, making a fire on the raft even though a fire was impossible, simply because survival demanded that they have a fire. In her dying years, Becky repeatedly called upon her husband to face the fact that she was dying, to talk with her about her suffering, and to quit insisting so foolishly and impotently that everything would be all right; his inability, or unwillingness, to do so drives her to desperation. "He loved his wife," Miss Welty tells us:

Whatever she did that she couldn't help doing was all right. Whatever she was driven to say was all right. But it was *not* all right! Her trouble was that very desperation. And no one had the power to cause that except the one she desperately loved, who refused to consider that she was desperate. It was betrayal on betrayal.

"Why did I marry a coward?" she asks him, as he stands helplessly by her bed:

"All you do is hurt me. I wish I might know what it is I've done. Why is it necessary to punish me like this and not tell me why?" And still she held fast to their hands, to Laurel's too. Her cry was not complaint; it was anger at wanting to know and being denied knowledge; it was love's deep anger.

Earlier, Miss Welty has told us that

Her father in his domestic gentleness had a horror of any sort of private clash, of divergence from the affectionate and the real and the explainable and the recognizable. He was a man of great delicacy; what he had not been born with he had learned in reaching toward his wife. He grimaced with delicacy. What he could not control was his belief that all his wife's troubles would turn out all right because there was nothing he would not have given her. When he reached a loss he simply put on his hat and went speechless out of the house to his office and worked for an hour or so getting up a brief for somebody.

Thus a man tough and competent and courageous in the world outside his home—he is a man, we are told at his funeral, who has single-handedly cowed a Ku Klux Klan mob on the courthouse steps—this courageous man cannot commit the act of love that his wife requires of him. He is, then, in marrying Fay, I would suggest, satisfying his need for companionship, but running from, avoiding, love's harsher demands. Fay's love is cheaply bought.

These painful memories of her parents' complex relationship conjured up for Laurel her relationship to her own husband, dead now for over two decades. In contrast to her parents' long and complicated lives together, her own marriage "had been of magical ease, of *ease*—of brevity and conclusion and all belonging to Chicago and not here"; "there had not happened a single blunder in their short life together." She and Phil simply had not lived together long enough to have developed either the kinds of problems or the kind of love that her mother and father had had, and therefore had not experienced either the kind of joy or the kind of pain. And we may well suspect that the reason she has not remarried is that the memories of the pain her parents had caused each other, long suppressed, were nevertheless real, and active. You may recall, in this connection, the passage in which Laurel remembers her grandmother's pigeons; they seem to me powerfully emblematic of the difficulties and paradoxes of love relationships that we have been talking about. Laurel remembers

a pair of them sticking their beaks down each other's throats, gagging each other, eating out of each other's craws, swallowing down all over again what had been swallowed before: they were taking turns. The first time, she hoped they might never do it again, but they did it again next day while the other pigeons copied them. They convinced her that they could not escape each other and could not themselves be escaped from. So when the pigeons flew down, she tried to position herself behind her grandmother's skirt, which was long and black, but her grandmother said again, "They're just hungry, like we are."

Laurel is panic-stricken at the sight, and I believe we are asked to see that the idea of human relationships conveyed in the pigeons' mutual devouring of each other is in large part the reason she has never remarried. Having had her marriage, now sealed off into its painless perfection and permanently preserved there, inviolate, she did not want to risk the possibility that another marriage, a longer-lasting one, would have required of her the same spiritual strength that her mother had required of her father. And so very like her optimist father, whose daughter she is, she has run from the entanglements of love, trying to save herself, though the experience of her mother's death has made her believe that no one can be saved, "Not from others." Her realization of this is rendered in what is for me one of the most moving passages in all of Miss Welty's work:

A flood of feeling descended on Laurel. She let the papers slide from her hand and the books from her knees, and put her head down on the open lid of the desk and wept in grief for love and for the dead. She lay there with all that was adamant in her yielding to this night, yielding at last. Now all she had found had found her. The deepest spring in her heart had uncovered itself, and it began to flow again.
If Phil could have lived—
But Phil was lost. Nothing of their life together remained except in her own memory; love was sealed away into its perfection and had remained there.
If Phil had lived—
She had gone on living with the old perfection undisturbed and undisturbing. Now, by her own hands, the past had been raised up, and *he* looked at her, Phil himself—here waiting, all the time, Lazarus. He looked at her out of eyes wild with the craving for his unlived life, with mouth open like a funnel's.
What would have been their end, then? Suppose their marriage had ended like her father and mother's? Or like her mother's father and mother's? Like—
"Laurel! Laurel! Laurel!" Phil's voice cried.
She wept for what happened to life.
"I wanted it!" Phil cried. His voice rose with the wind in the

night and went around the house and around the house. It became a roar. "I wanted it!"

Now, having missed it, Laurel wishes she had had it.

It is an adolescent view that looks upon love as a problem-solver, that says, in effect, if I could just break down that barrier, if I could just find somebody to return the love that I have to give, my life would be much better, simpler; I would be much happier. Miss Welty knows that it simply doesn't work that way—that love not only alters when it alteration finds, but it actively seeks out alterations to make. Love always creates more problems than it ever solves, because love entails relationship, and relationship entails responsibility, and responsibility entails a loss of freedom. And that loss of freedom, however willingly we accept it and bear it, is all too frequently a heavy burden. It is the high price we pay for family and friends and love: without which we would all be like Tom Harris—free, and helpless.

A Form of Thanks

REYNOLDS PRICE

SOME OF YOU MAY KNOW that I've already said a good deal about Eudora Welty, in print and in public. I've written a long essay called "The Onlooker, Smiling," which looks at the whole of her work in the bright light thrown by *The Optimist's Daughter*. You can find the essay in a book of mine called *Things Themselves*. Beyond that, I've spoken and written both about her work and about the value of her work for my own; the value of her encouraging friendship, which began blessedly when I was a college senior, twenty-two years ago.

In fact, I've said so much about Eudora Welty—and all of it so nearly monotonous with praise—that when Louis Dollarhide kindly invited me to come to this symposium, I told him (A) that I accepted with pleasure and honor and (B) that when it came to the question of my presenting a formal paper, I felt a good deal like a character in *The Optimist's Daughter*: the old woman in the hospital who says, "I declare, I'm getting to where I ain't got much left to say to Dad myself." And my *memory* is that I asked Louis to think of something for me to do besides make a speech. He said he would. Time passed. The program arrived a while ago, and you will now know as well as I that what he thought of was—*3 p.m.: Reynolds Price, A Novelist's View.* Thank you, Louis.

Faced with that, I considered—what *was* the novelist's view, when the novelist's view was simple and had been given, again and again? A number of possibilities dawned, mostly desperate. I even suggested to Eudora that I might show my slides from last summer's trip to Austria—"the novelist's view," of something new at least. Eudora said "*Sure.*" But I lost my nerve.

So—what I mean to do is, first, to give briefly again this one novelist's view of Eudora Welty's work and then to give you a sample of one of the kinds of work her work has been helpful in generating, one example of her extraordinary power not only as a creator but as a germinatrix.

My view is this—and she's going to hate my saying it; she always chides me when I praise her—Eudora Welty's fiction is the richest in human understanding and in power to shape and convey that understanding of any living writer known to me. In all of American fiction, she stands for me with her only peers—Melville, James, Hemingway, and Faulkner—and among them, she is in some crucial respects the deepest, the most spacious, the most lifegiving.

It is one aspect of that *lifegivingness* that I'd like to expand on a little before giving my promised demonstration of one of the effects of her work.

It is famous that a great artist is not necessarily a good influence, even a fruitful example, for his immediate—or distant—successors. John Milton, a writer whom I love passionately, is the notorious older example of such a genius; one who laid a chill hand on his successors for two centuries after. The great citizen of this town may be our most interesting modern example of such a writer—a genius whose vision, knowledge, and intensity were so personal, so individual as to leave his works objects of wonder more than of emulation or of forward guidance.

It is one of the supererogatory virtues of Eudora Welty's work, however, that it has provided—with all its central gifts—one by no means negligible gift: the gift of hope and instruction for another generation of American writers. A Southern male novelist, slightly my elder, has spoken of her as "The Matrix of us all." By *all* he meant all the Southern writers younger than she; and while the claim is sweeping, I would gladly concede that it is almost entirely true. Of course, one must caution a roomful of literary scholars to remember that a good writer's work is ever and always made, first and last, from *life* and not from other books—that life which boiled round, under, and above a writer from the moment of birth and which has permanently shaped and aimed him years before he begins to read even *Mother Goose*.

But Eudora Welty—in the wide centrality of her vision, in her fixed yet nimble scrutiny of what might tritely be called "the normal world" (the normal daily world of the vast country called the American South) and in the nearly infinite resourcefulness with which she has found means to convey the discoveries of that scrutiny—has opened to a whole generation of writers the simple but nearly unattainable possibility of *work*. We read her fiction, we recognized our world, we knew that our world was therefore the possible source of more good fiction. It had been done once; it could now be done again, and differently.

So we've done it again, with our own various results. Flannery O'Connor, Truman Capote, Toni Morrison, Reynolds Price, Anne Tyler (to name only five) are writers who would surely have been different writers, though not necessarily worse, if they had lacked the large but warmly accessible example of books like *A Curtain of Green*, *The Wide Net*, *Delta Wedding*, *The Golden Apples*. And the fact that our own work was well underway—and in one case tragically completed—before the triumphant *Losing Battles* and *The Optimist's Daughter* has only increased for most of us the power of her guidance: an American writer has at last produced a third act in her career—an act unimaginably better than its own great predecessors. And she continues to promise more.

I think I have the right to thank her again—here publicly, for myself and for others—for that. If I don't have the right, then I've just usurped it.

And may I make that thanks in the form of a poem?—a poem which I wrote seven years ago but have recently revised. It is not a poem *about* Eudora Welty or her work. It was neither directly inspired by nor, I think, influenced by any specific work of hers. Yet, if I may speak personally for an instant, it is a poem which balances upon that single broad but high theme which I believe her work and my work to share—the theme which, as a boy of fourteen, I sighted in the first story of hers I read ("A Worn Path") and which I at once recognized as my own truest knowledge, my own deepest need.

Since you are all licensed detectives—and since Eudora herself is one of the Western world's most voracious consumers of mysteries—I won't state the theme. If I could state it, obviously I wouldn't have written the poem. It is called "To My Niece—Our Photograph in a Hammock."

No one thinks you are mine.
I could have bought you from gypsies

Or—desperate, if solitude had left me desperate—
From a defrocked doctor who bootlegs at night,
With abortions and morphine, a sideline of babies:
A derelict blond blue-eyed bastard
In my Black-Welsh arms.

They're wrong—you are.
At eighteen months (a day, a moment),
You are my remains, my physical remains;
And you hoard already, little banker (no choice),
In dense dry ovaries, green pomegranates,
Every egg you will ever pay out on speculation,
Four hundred maybe in your fertile years.
Each one, of thousands—you are chocked, for safety;
Roed like a shad against loneliness, extinction—
Guards already in final form, unknown as your death,
Some of the instructions I might have passed to Man:
A collateral share of my parents at least,
My share of parents extending to Adam.

Man may yet do without them.
If our picture is omen, you may seal your vaults,
Say the monthly No to the monthly hope,
Balk every try at blind continuance;
For though, in the frame, my hands strain to hold you,
Transmit a few things I know,
You struggle to escape—me; your volunteering life
That swells each instant in you, presses every wall—
And you laugh, not with me but elsewhere, outward.
I know in retrospect that you laugh at the sky
Northwest of my roof, but what decked the sky
For you that day?—that evening, evening light.

What vision? What clear shaft opening to joy?
Like a white baby seal—a dugong calf!—
You paddle the June air around us toward freedom.

I am laughing for the cameraman (your laughing father)
So I do not notice—and wouldn't mind.
Here, I have you safely—my arms vs. yours—
And if, in years, your struggles wrench you loose,
Award you solitude, sterility, space,
The world will return you (in hunger or duty—
It has brought me to you; I am choosing to hold you);
Trap you, raving, gnashing; feed you its diet.

Look. Neither of us noticed the news of that day—
You rapt in babyhood, I in pleasure—
The bedrock above which we hung and giggled.
Our picture, pitiless monitor, preserves it:
Even the hammock we swing in is a net.

Eudora Welty:
A Friend's View

CHARLOTTE CAPERS

AT THE END—AND ALSO THE HIGHEST
point—of this most successful symposium, I want to pre-
pare you for a sudden change of pace. I share with you the
admiration, veneration, and awe that a woman of Eudora
Welty's genius inspires. However, my assignment—
Eudora Welty: A Friend's View (in ten minutes)—pre-
cludes further scholarly contemplation. Rather, I will try
to convey to you something of the feeling of joy and glad-
ness that comes from knowing Eudora as a friend.

My assignment is a pleasant one. I have "viewed" Eudora as a friend since 1946, when, as a moonlighting reporter for the *Jackson Daily News*, I interviewed her
about the popular success of her first full-length novel,
Delta Wedding. Before 1946 I had viewed Eudora as an
acquaintance, an interesting person, a fellow Jacksonian
of whom I was very proud. After our 1946 meeting I joined
that vast and distinguished company, Friends of Eudora
Welty, to whose ranks I still belong.

From 1946 until about 1966, when the vicissitudes of
life began to thin our ranks, I was the happy member of a
group of eight friends and neighbors in Jackson, including
Eudora, who met regularly on birthdays and other special
occasions, to break bread together, to wine and dine, and

to celebrate. We had dinner together almost every week to celebrate almost anything: the opening of a moon flower by the light of a harvest moon; parties of greeting and welcome to Eudora's steady stream of friends from out of state; parties of parting when some of us went on trips; and especially parties on birthdays. The moon flower party stands out in my memory—I can almost see the flower on the moon vine opening, trembling open, right on schedule for our group, as we stood around in the moonlight on a cool fall night. Almost as spectacular, in a different way, was the party where we tried a new method of cooking roast beef, which required that the roast be packed in ice cream salt and wrapped in thirty-two layers of wet newspaper before being buried in hot coals on a barbecue pit. This turned out to be an impossible task unless the host and hostess got into the bathtub with the roast, which they did, on this occasion. Needless to say, that was the last of the roast parties, but the memory lingers on.

On these occasions we were moved by the muse of poetry—perhaps the same muse that inspired Edna Earle to write the poem "Come Back to Clay"—to burst into verse. And in the very few minutes I have allotted to me, I think perhaps you can get something of the feeling of our palmy days from some of our festival odes.

In 1970 *Losing Battles* was published, and I suppose that our little home group was more involved with *Losing Battles* than with anything else that Eudora has done. Eudora does not like to discuss her work on social occasions, and our conversation is usually general. But I believe that our group, by then firmly established in our own minds as the Basic Eight, was able to make a contribution to Eudora's book by suggesting names for characters in her story, taken from life. Eudora's characters have marvelous names, as you know, and some of them may have been contributed by the Basic Eight. I remember Eudora's absolute delight when a name struck her as just right for a character she had in mind. Aunt Birdie. Lexie. Bonnie Dee and Johnny Ree. Lady May. Teacake Magee. Edna Earle. Etoyle and Brother Bethune. At any rate, *Losing Battles* was in progress over a long period of time, and we had talked about it with Eudora, usually in regard to names. So we had a special interest in it, and when the book was published, the Basic Eight thought a celebration was in order. For the occasion we had a small gold pin made for Eudora, inscribed "Losing Battles." Our menu was an effort to duplicate the family reunion menu in *Losing Battles*. One of our number designed a banner for the entrance hall, inscribed with a quotation from the book, "I call this a Reunion to remember, all!" And it was. When the feasting was done, we offered a verse.

On this glad reunion day
Each of us will have our say.
First, our thanks to Granny Vaughan
Who, at ninety, brought this on.
All our love to The Eudora
Now, as always, we adore her.
The light of fame Eudo reflects
Set us to cooking chicken necks.
Remember this reunion, all,
Don't let Miss Julia cast a pall.
And gather 'round the birthday cake
And from Jack Renfro wisdom take.
Don't give anybody up or leave anybody out,
That's what love is all about.
No test of love should prove too risky
For good old friends preserved in whisky.

That may give you a rough idea of the high intellectual plane of our meetings!

As Eudora continued her steady progression through medals, awards, honors, and degrees, she naturally inspired more bursts of—I don't know that we could call it poetry—and on her birthday, in 1972, we celebrated her winning of the Gold Medal for Literature from the American Academy of Arts and Letters. Here—in Oxford—it should be remembered that when William Faulkner was awarded the Gold Medal for Literature from the American Academy of Arts and Letters, it was his fellow Mississippian Eudora Welty who presented the medal to him. Now, in 1972, Katherine Anne Porter was to present the medal to Eudora. So we took note of this, as follows:

As we celebrate our betters
Honored by the American Academy of Arts and Letters
We think about April thirteen
Of which Miss Welty is undisputed queen.
Now Miss Welty takes the stand
To get the medal from Katherine Anne.
. . .
Happy birthday, Gold Medal Winner,
You DESERVE a birthday dinner.
Prophetess: WITH honor HERE
Your own country—finds you dear.

In 1973, with the Pulitzer Prize, and Jackson's pride in Eudora bursting, the Board of Directors of the Mississippi Arts Festival, Inc., asked the Governor to declare an official Eudora Welty Day in Mississippi. This resulted in a memorable day in honor of Eudora, which I think was really one of the high points in her life—one of the times she enjoyed and appreciated most. Her friends from all over this country, and some from out of this country, were invited to come to Jackson to honor her. And to her joy and, being Eudora, to her surprise, they came! It was a wonderful day, with felicitous ceremonies and elegant parties, and Eudora's friends at home and abroad merrily intermingling. So, of course, when the captains and the kings departed, the old basic group met, and commemorated Eudora Welty and her Day, in rhyme.

Decked out like a potentate
In honors we all celebrate.
A medal here, a trophy there,
She wears with quite a casual air.
The creator of Uncle Daniel
Is friendly as a cocker spaniel.
The maker-up of Edna Earle
Is most at home on the River Pearl.
Dear Eudora, Adoremus!
We are proud to have you claim us.
Friends we've been and friends we'll stay
Long past Eudora Welty Day!

I am proud to say that I own the only letter Eudora Welty ever wrote to a dog. This letter, or card, was written to my dog Holly, an impatient wire-haired terrier, who was very much a participant in the doings of the Basic Eight. Holly became pregnant, and her pregnancy was of great interest to us all. Eudora had to go to New York when Holly's accouchement was due, so was not able to be with us for the birthing, at which Holly was delivered, or delivered herself, of eight puppies. Eudora wrote Holly twice. The first letter, written when the puppies were born, was entitled, "Keep Smiling, Holly." The note read:

Holly, you are just the BERRIES!
YOU thought PET MILK came from DAIRIES.
Though eight puppies is no LAUGH
What WOULD BE SAD is EIGHT AND A HALF!
Love, EW.

In spite of this encouragement, Holly found motherhood a bore, and went into post-natal depression. So another word came to her, addressed "Holly, c/o Miss Charlotte Capers, Department of Archives and History, War Memorial Building, Jackson, Mississippi": "Dear Holly. This is from your doctor. Listen, don't call me, I'll call you. MY hours are at a PREMIUM. Please don't get excited, SMILE, and the next time, *think*."

I will be forgiven, I hope, for reading an inscription written by Eudora on the title page of a book she gave me for one of *my* birthdays. The book was *The Elements of Style*, by William S. Strunk, Jr., and E. B. White, and in it Eudora wrote:

All the elements of style
Belong already to this chile
And may she never get the vapors
Said E. B. White of Charlotte Capers.
Happy Birthday, 1972, with love from Eudora.

I hope that these fragments from a long association will

suggest that there has been "laughter and the love of friends" all along the way for Eudora.

Now, this will be the last reading from *my* works. Here is another birthday ode, written to commemorate Eudora's most recent accolade—the honorary degree of doctor of humane letters from Harvard. It is called "To Eudora, on her Birthday, April 13, 1977."

Off the lecture circuit hot
She flies to us from Agnes Scott.
From Endowment for the Arts
She rushes off to foreign parts.
Laude cum and magna cum—
She will need a trophy room.
For doctor this and doctor that
On skin of sheep and mortar hat.
And now—with Harvard's crimson nod
She leaves us for the bean and cod.
Ultimate! and ultimatum!
Jubilate! Jubilatum!
Happy Birthday, dear Eudora,
Our Magnolia Grandiflora!

It gives me a great deal of pride and pleasure to present to you Eudora Welty.

List of Contributors

CLEANTH BROOKS, Sterling Professor Emeritus of English and Gray Professor Emeritus of Rhetoric at Yale University, has taught and lectured at colleges and universities in America and abroad. With Robert Penn Warren he founded *The Southern Review* at Louisiana State University and wrote the epoch-making *Understanding Poetry* and its successors *Understanding Fiction* and *Understanding Drama*. Brooks is author of other celebrated works, including *Modern Poetry and the Tradition, The Well Wrought Urn, A Shaping Joy: Studies in the Writer's Craft*, and two volumes on William Faulkner's works. Essays on his remarkable achievements as teacher and critic have been brought together in a book edited by Lewis P. Simpson, *The Possibilities of Order: Cleanth Brooks and His Work*.

CHARLOTTE CAPERS has been a close friend of Eudora Welty since 1946 when, as a reporter for the *Jackson Daily News*, she interviewed the writer about the popular success of her first full-length novel, *Delta Wedding*. Her special association with other Welty works includes playing the part of Edna Earle in an early production of *The Ponder Heart* and assisting with the publication of a limited

136

edition of the *Fairy Tale of the Natchez Trace*. Charlotte Capers directed the Mississippi Department of Archives and History for fourteen years and now serves as director of its Division of Information and Education.

MICHAEL KREYLING is currently on leave from Mississippi State University to serve as Mellon Postdoctoral Fellow in English at Tulane University. He chose for his thesis at Cornell University *The Novels of Eudora Welty*, and he has written articles on her works for *Mississippi Quarterly* and *The Southern Review*. Kreyling also contributed "An Introduction to Eudora Welty" to the Mississippi Library Commission's pamphlet series.

NOEL POLK, who teaches at the University of Southern Mississippi, is a contributing editor of the *Eudora Welty Newsletter* and has written numerous works on Welty and other Mississippi authors. He recently published an edition of William Faulkner's *Marionettes* and is currently compiling a Welty bibliography and an anthology of Mississippi writers.

PEGGY W. PRENSHAW, Honors Professor of English at the University of Southern Mississippi, is editor of *Southern Quarterly* and has published a number of articles on Eudora Welty, Tennessee Williams, and other Southern writers. She is currently editing *Eudora Welty: Collected Essays*, to be published in 1979 by the University Press of Mississippi.

REYNOLDS PRICE, Angier B. Duke Professor of English at Duke University, is a poet, short-story writer, novelist, and essayist. His books include *A Long and Happy Life*, which received the award of the William Faulkner Foundation for a notable first novel, *The Names and Faces of Heroes*, *A Generous Man*, *Love and Work*, *Permanent Errors*, and *The Surface of Earth*. Two essays on Eudora Welty are included in his collection *Things Themselves: Essays and Scenes*.

WILLIAM JAY SMITH has written six volumes of poetry for adults, a dozen volumes of poetry for children, two books of essays, television scripts, and a comedy, *The Straw Market*. He has also edited five poetry anthologies and translated six volumes of French, Russian, Italian, Spanish, and Hungarian poetry. Among his best known books are *The Tin Can and Other Poems*, *New and Selected Poems*, and *The Streaks of the Tulip, Selected Criticism*. He has conducted writers' conferences, served as consultant on poetry to the Library of Congress, and lectured in many parts of the United States and abroad.

www.ingramcontent.com/pod-product-compliance
Lightning Source LLC
Chambersburg PA
CBHW020700030726
47498CB00002B/590